W9-DBI-201

IN THE MOOD FOR *Munsingwear*

IN THE MOOD FOR Munsingwear®

MINNESOTA'S CLAIM TO UNDERWEAR FAME

Susan Marks

MINNESOTA HISTORICAL SOCIETY PRESS

CANCEL

The publication of this book was supported, in part, by a gift from the Bean Family Fund for Business History.

© 2011 by Susan Marks. All rights reserved. No part of this book may be used or reproduced in any manner whatsoever without written permission except in the case of brief quotations embodied in critical articles and reviews. For information, write to the Minnesota Historical Society Press, 345 Kellogg Blvd. W., St. Paul, MN 55102–1906.

The Munsingwear® trademarks and logos are owned by PEI Licensing, Inc., a wholly owned subsidiary of Perry Ellis International, Inc. All rights reserved. This book was created and published without verification of facts or approval by PEI Licensing, Inc.

www.mhspress.org

The Minnesota Historical Society Press is a member of the Association of American University Presses.

Manufactured in Canada

10 9 8 7 6 5 4 3 2 1

♾ The paper used in this publication meets the minimum requirements of the American National Standard for Information Sciences—Permanence for Printed Library Materials, ANSI Z39.48-1984.

International Standard Book Number
ISBN: 978-0-87351-822-2 (cloth)

LIBRARY OF CONGRESS CATALOGING-IN-PUBLICATION DATA
Marks, Susan.
    In the mood for Munsingwear : Minnesota's claim to underwear fame / Susan Marks.
        p. cm.
    Includes bibliographical references and index.
    ISBN 978-0-87351-822-2 (cloth : alk. paper)
    1. Munsingwear, Inc. (U.S.) 2. Underwear—Minnesota—History. I. Title.
    TT670.M29 2011
    646.4'209776—dc22   2010050278

In the Mood for Munsingwear was designed and set in type by Christopher Kuntze.
The text type is Whitman with Liza Pro and Engraver's Gothic for display.
Printed and bound by Friesens, Manitoba, Canada.

To Jane Marks-Hastig, my sister,
whose unrestricted support surpasses that
of any push-up bra

CONTENTS

PREFACE

Underwear is tricky. You express a little healthy interest in the clothes under there, and the next thing you know, you've got a reputation. While conducting research for this book I was regularly referred to as "the underwear lady" and the "panty preacher" (although the latter was by my sister, so maybe it doesn't count). One well-intending blogger even announced to the entire Internet that I wanted people "to get excited about old underwear."

I wouldn't call myself an underwear enthusiast, exactly, but there's no denying that I've spent more time thinking about underwear than the average person.

My professional relationship with underwear began when I was hired in the mid-1990s to work in the "Intimate Apparel Department" at the Dayton Hudson Department Store in downtown Minneapolis. As far as retail gigs go, this one wasn't half bad. It was genuinely pleasant to work among the most intimate of apparels.

I engaged in thoughtful conversations with cross-dressers about foundation wear and its merits of form over function, and the other way around. I observed the rite of passage of mothers and daughters awkwardly shopping together for "training" bras. I helped a few embarrassed young men shop for their girlfriends. (And no, they never asked me to try anything on for them.) Once I even ran interference for a bride-to-be who was having a meltdown in the dressing room while she contemplated her future. And the best part? I amassed a collection of underwear so impressive that it made my fiancé forget that I was spending part of our honeymoon fund.

Years later, I got another underwear-related job—this time with the Minnesota Historical Society. I worked as a costumed tour guide at the Alexander Ramsey House, a Victorian mansion in St. Paul. On an average day I wore a corset, bustle, and two layers of petticoats beneath my Victorian gown. I skipped a few layers, like a chemise and drawers, opting for modern-day underwear. Thank goodness none of the tourists checked beneath my skirt for historical accuracy. The same cannot be said for another costumed guide in an incident that has become legendary around the Minnesota Historical Society.

Around the time I was parading around in my Victorian work uniform, I was also a graduate student at the University of Minnesota, where I worked as a professor's assistant in the Department of Design, Housing, and Apparel. I was surrounded by colleagues who talked brilliantly about the sociology of dress. But it was the quirkiest and most controversial aspects of dress that captivated me. I told anyone who would listen about the Minnesota Historical Society's collection of underwear—the largest underwear collection in the Midwest—consisting mostly of Munsingwear underwear. The collection, donated to the society in the early 1980s, when the company shut down its factory in North Minneapolis, included thirty-five hundred garments, along with company papers, photos, salesmen's samples, and premiums.

Munsingwear was particularly fascinating to me because it cultivated a squeaky-clean, wholesome image with its union suits and golf shirts—but at the same time, the company had a history of advertising that was, occasionally, the opposite of wholesome. I wanted to know more about this underwear icon, and it was just a matter of time before I allowed myself to be wrapped up in Munsingwear's union suits, chemises, silk stockings, bras, briefs, and half-slips.

For decades we've lived with the notion that near nudity is nothing shocking, but if you say the word *panties,* you will get people's undivided attention. And the company played a historic role in our uneasy relationship with underwear. Munsingwear was once the largest manufacturer of underwear in the United States, outselling the competition and getting up close and personal with millions of Americans' private parts. There's something so intriguing and even taboo about the thin layer of fabric closest to our skin. Even after all these years of *nothing shocking*, we just can't seem to shake the hold underwear has on us. And we probably never will.

IN THE MOOD FOR *Munsingwear*

1 UNMENTIONABLE

George Munsing, the father
of itchless underwear

IN THE 1890s, polite society wouldn't dream of hanging women's and men's underwear together on the same clothesline, let alone openly discuss this forbidden under-fabric. Yet underwear manufacturers like Minnesota's Northwestern Knitting Company found it impossible to advertise their wares without showing their unmentionables. So they did—carefully, with photographs of garments lying flat, with images of women holding underwear. But in what the company claimed as a historic first, Northwestern Knitting's ad in an 1897 issue of *Ladies' Home Journal* showed a photograph of a little girl actually wearing a union suit—and the text promised, "Ask your dealer for our *free Booklet* showing styles *photographed* on *living models,* or address The Northwestern Knitting Co., Minneapolis, Minn." With this, the company urged the nation to step a little closer to the provocative world that lies beneath.

This ad in the September 1897 issue of *Ladies' Home Journal* may have been America's first underwear advertisement showing a live model.

Itchless

Minnesota's claim to underwear fame began in 1886 when George D. Munsing moved from New York to Minnesota with underwear on his mind—specifically, itchless underwear. Winter wool long underwear, a necessity in cold climates, was an item of torture for millions who simply could not tolerate the feel of wool

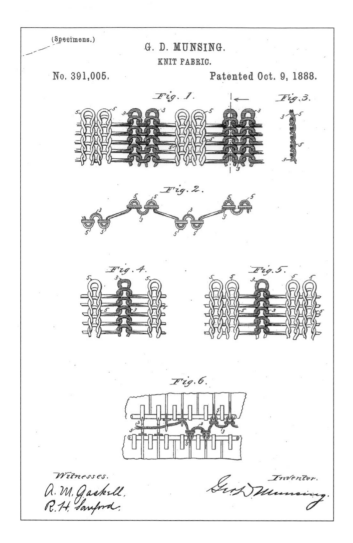

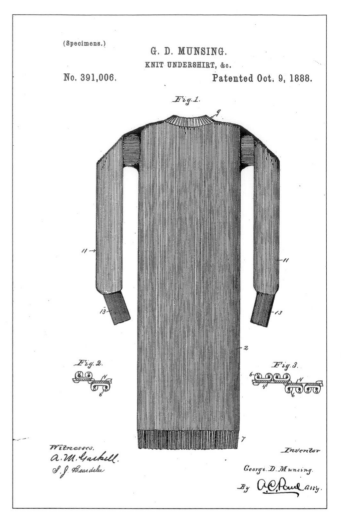

against their skin. Munsing, while a superintendent at the Rochester Knitting Works in New York, invented an ingenious process to plate silk on wool, thus creating a fabric that was warm yet would not irritate the skin. Together with his two associates from the Massachusetts Institute of Technology, Frank H. Page and Edward O. Tuttle, Munsing founded the Northwest Knitting Company. (The company would eventually change its name to Munsingwear, to match its brand.) They set up shop in a rented warehouse, the Reese Storage Building, on the outskirts of the flour milling district of Minneapolis.

Sales were surprisingly brisk, and within a year, the company moved again, this time renting space in the Dodson-Fisher-Brockman saddlery building. The

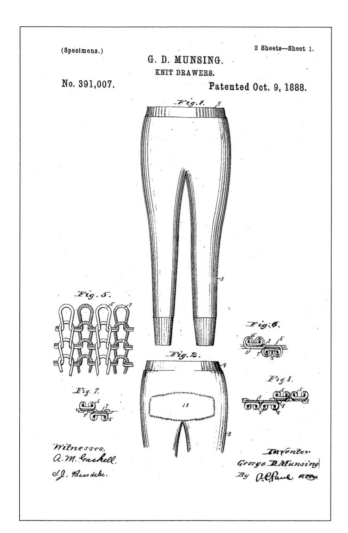

(Specimens.)

G. D. MUNSING.
KNIT DRAWERS.

No. 391,007.

2 Sheets—Sheet 1.

Patented Oct. 9, 1888.

Fig.1.

Fig.5.

Fig.6.

Fig.7.

Fig.2.

Fig.8.

Witnesses,
A. M. Gaskell.
S. J. Beardsley.

Inventor
George D. Munsing
By A. C. Paul atty

Munsing's patents for the silk-plated "double-ribbed jersey fabric" knitted of silk and wool and the garments he made with it. In this process, silk thread was passed through the fabric from one side to the other, covering the wool so that it did not touch the skin, to provide itch-free but warm undergarments.

businessmen incorporated, with their patent attorney, Amasa C. Paul, serving as president, Munsing as vice president, Tuttle as secretary, and Page as treasurer. Northwestern Knitting expanded its underwear offerings to include various kinds of Munsing's patented underwear in an array of colors and styles for men, women, and children.

Munsing handled all the technological aspects while his partners ran the company—almost into the ground. For the first few years, supply collided with demand at the Northwestern Knitting Company. Customers clamored for the new itchless underwear, but the company failed to deliver on the modern marvel it had advertised.

Expanding rapidly in its early years, the Northwest Knitting Company kept outgrowing its factories. This building at 213 Lyndale Avenue North became its fourth home in five years in 1891.

Two employees pose with the steam engines that powered the mill, about 1900.

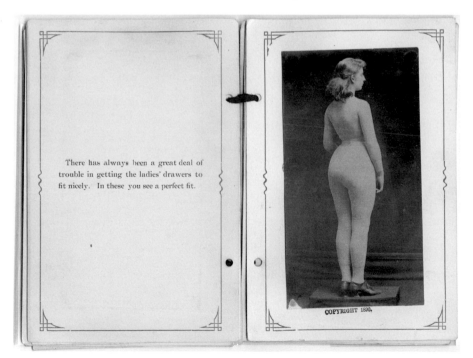

There has always been a great deal of trouble in getting the ladies' drawers to fit nicely. In these you see a perfect fit.

COPYRIGHT 1890,

Munsingwear was everywhere, including on this parade float for Singer's, an Oklahoma clothing store that specialized in Munsingwear union suits. This image was made into a postcard around 1908.

In the 1890s, salesmen carried catalogs with original photographic prints to show clothing-store buyers their underwear options.

Deadlines for shipping were missed and customers were charged for orders not received. As in all traditional textile factories, the majority of the work was done on knitting and sewing machines, but because Northwestern Knitting was committed to a "perfect fit," many orders had to be custom made and required sewing and knitting by hand. Additionally, every dropped stitch had to be resewn and every tail thread trimmed. The pace and attention to detail were almost impossible to maintain.

Telegrams and letters of discontent arrived from all over the nation:

> If goods are not sent this week, don't ship, been disappointed
> enough. Now answer!
> Daughter must have goods this week, cannot wait long!
> Letter received won't keep people warm—ship at once.
> It's too late now. Cancel order.
> Our whole family had to lay [sic] in bed till our undershirts were
> washed and all because you haven't sent us any new ones.

Employees scrambled to fill as many orders as possible, but these were dark days, and the company's fate hung in the balance. Salvation came in 1887, with strong financial backing from world-famous flour miller Charles A. Pillsbury, Minneapolis banker Clinton Morrison, and transportation tycoon Thomas Lowry, all of whom served on the board of directors and whose purchase of stock in the company provided much-needed capital.

To keep up with the ever-growing demand for long underwear, undershirts, ladies' under vests, and more, Northwestern Knitting temporarily subcontracted with several other textile mills and set up a sales and distribution office in New York. Still, the company faced many problems, not the least of which was bad press airing Munsingwear's own dirty laundry.

Letters from retailers and individuals poured into the company's offices— including praise for itchless underwear, orders for more of it, and complaints when it didn't arrive.

Journalist Eva McDonald
Valesh, a.k.a. Eva Gay, who
went undercover in several
Twin Cities factories to expose
unfair labor practices, shown
here in about 1886

Eva Gay

From 1888 to 1891, Twin Cities labor activist and journalist Eva McDonald
Valesh wrote for the *St. Paul Globe* under the pen name Eva Gay. She often
went undercover to expose poor working conditions and unfair labor practices,
especially for women. Gay reported her findings in a *Globe* series called "Eva
Gay's Travels."

Nicollet Avenue and Third Street, Minneapolis, on a winter day in 1886, when woolen underwear was a necessity of life

Gay frequently took her meals at boardinghouses to get the latest work-related news and new leads from women laborers. Sometimes she engaged in these conversations; at other times, she eavesdropped. In a Minneapolis boardinghouse in 1888, she overheard a woman say that she wished Eva Gay would come to the Northwestern Knitting Company and "tell how we are treated and what wages we get. If she found all there was to say it would make better reading than anything she told yet."

Before this, the journalist had heard nothing but favorable things about the new Northwestern Knitting Company. Determined to find out more, Gay walked right into the factory, up the stairs, and into a large workroom—essentially hiding in plain sight to conduct her investigative reporting. She immediately noted the lack of air circulation and deemed the work environment "unwholesome." She also noticed the factory was dirty—but no dirtier than any other textile factory she had visited.

Gay observed the forelady taking what food she wanted from the lunches of the women on her crew, who were too afraid to protest. After the forelady left, Gay questioned "the girls" about sharing their lunches, noting, "The girls didn't smile at all; they looked as though they had something to say, but felt a little doubtful about saying it." Gay played dumb and praised the forelady for her friendliness until one worker finally spoke up: "That's what she does; she doesn't ever say please, but takes what she fancies, seeming to think that the compliment is all on our side." Gay noted to her readers that if the forelady ever helped herself to Gay's lunch, she would make sure it was a meal that would "spoil her appetite for a week or so."

The crew reported to Gay that they weren't allowed to talk, sing, laugh, or eat while working. Their male overseer, rumored to be a former slave driver from the antebellum South, threatened to paint over the windows if he caught them gazing outside during work hours.

One of the biggest abuses Gay unveiled was the unfair and inconsistent manner in which work was distributed to employees. Each worker was paid by the garment, or "piece," yet these women might have to sit around for hours—unpaid—waiting for garments to be assigned to them.

Gay carefully took notes about the unfair labor practices at the Northwestern Knitting Company. One worker warned Gay that the overseer, who made sure the "girls don't carry the factory home," would surely confiscate her notebook. But Gay slipped out unnoticed and spread the word about the injustices that took place behind the closed doors of the Northwestern Knitting factory.

The first of five buildings that became the company's complex on 718 Western Avenue, built in 1904, was also the first reinforced concrete building in Minneapolis. This structure housed the general offices, medical departments, and boxing, labeling, and stock rooms.

If Gay's exposé wasn't a wake-up call to Northwestern Knitting Company, the growing discontent among garment workers nationwide certainly got the company's attention. Between 1880 and 1920, the needle trade was the country's third-most strike-prone industry after the mining and building trades. Garment workers were unionizing and revolting against unfair wages, unsafe working conditions, and long hours.

The most prominent needle trade union, the International Ladies' Garment Workers' Union (ILGWU), was formed in 1900 in New York City out of seven smaller needle trade unions. In 1909, the ILGWU made headlines around the world with "The Uprising of the 20,000." A relatively small group of garment workers walked off the job at the Triangle Waist Company (often called the Triangle Shirtwaist Company), sparking thousands of others across the city to follow suit in a fourteen-week strike. Very little was resolved by the strike, and another, larger strike, "The Great Revolt," took place a few months later. The ILGWU led this massive strike of sixty thousand workers, which lasted several months and resulted in higher wages for workers and a basic health benefits package.

The strikes ushered in violence and arrests in New York City, as well as in Chicago, Cleveland, and Philadelphia, where similar large strikes soon followed. Still, sweatshops flourished in garment districts, and relations between manufacturers and employees were perpetually strained.

The injustices against garment workers led to one of the greatest tragedies in U.S. labor history. On March 25, 1911, a fire broke out in the Triangle Waist Company factory in New York, causing the death of 146 workers and injuries to 71 mostly young, immigrant women. Some of the workers were as young as fifteen years old.

Many of the five hundred workers could not escape the burning building because management had locked the doors to the stairwells and exits to deter workers from stealing from the company. The ladders on fire trucks could not reach the workers on the highest floors, nor could the water from the fire hoses. Witnesses watched in horror as desperate women leaped to their deaths.

In Minnesota, the Northwestern Knitting Company's managers didn't want anything to do with the problems that plagued other garment factories. A new fire-proof factory was under construction, and to help avoid unionization and strikes, and to lower turnover, they opted to improve the company on their own terms. It was several years before Northwestern shook its sweatshop image, solved its efficiency and management problems, and got a handle on marketing its products, but when it did, the results were nothing short of remarkable.

2 What's Under There?

Ad, ca. 1919. The
Northwestern Knitting
Company often portrayed
the Munsingwear brand as
a family affair.

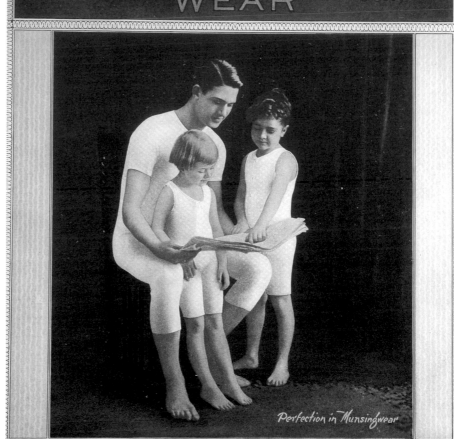

A DISTINGUISHED SERVICE LABEL

PERFECT
FITTING

MUNSING WEAR

UNION
SUITS

Perfection in Munsingwear

MUNSINGWEAR FOR MEN, WOMEN, CHILDREN

Fine in Quality—Non-irritating—Long Wearing—Perfect Fitting—in every way Satisfactory

Because Munsingwear fits and covers the form so perfectly, is such a wonder in the wash as well as wear, and gives such all 'round Union Suit service and satisfaction, millions of men, women, children, always say Munsingwear—and never ask for underwear. "Light as a feather," summer Munsingwear Union Suits in sheer, cool fabrics weigh only a few ounces. Reaching, running, standing, sitting, Munsingwear is always perfect fitting. It's a Munsingwear habit to outwash, outwear, outlast expectations. Munsingwear is made in many different styles, sizes, fabrics, both light and medium weight. Men's athletic suits may be had in both form fitting knitted fabrics and loose fitting woven garments accurately sized and carefully finished. No matter the size of your person or purse there's an up to date dealer in every city or town of importance in the United States who can Union Suit you with Munsingwear.

NEVER ASK FOR UNDERWEAR-ALWAYS SAY MUNSINGWEAR

THE NORTHWESTERN KNITTING COMPANY became so closely identified with the union suit that many believed that Munsing was its inventor, but this simply wasn't so. Union suits, first developed in the late 1860s, united the top and bottom of underwear into a one-piece, snug-fitting undergarment. The union suit was the solution to the common complaint of exposed skin in cold climates whenever people bent over, reached, or stretched. In the days before advancements in home and workplace heating, this was no idle complaint, even more so for outside laborers. Most union suits buttoned up the front and had an "access hatch," or button-up flap, in the back, so the union suit wearer didn't need to disrobe completely to use the toilet.

Munsing and his company took this warm, practical union suit concept and made their own version, complete with the patented Munsingwear fabric and fit, and it outsold all the competition. The reasonably priced Munsingwear union suit became the company's signature garment, and its popularity lasted for decades.

Advertising Under There

Early Munsingwear ads for union suits were far from risqué, but they did show imagery of people in underwear, running the risk of alienating potential customers who found *any* underwear advertising crass and an affront to Victorian modesty. The company's famous slogan, "Don't Say Underwear, Say Munsingwear," was at first followed by "It's More Refined." This was a genuflection of sorts to the past while it moved forward on a new underwear frontier—mass print advertising.

Ladies' Home Journal, 1917. Union suits weren't the only thing covering the ladies in Munsingwear ads; flower bouquets often made a demure appearance.

To lure customers into the warm embrace of Munsingwear suits, the company advertised with tasteful imagery of family scenes. Intended to evoke a sense of serenity and security, these ads showed underwear-clad families relaxing in the sanctity of home. At the same time, the ads were voyeuristic portals into a fantasy world where families comfortably lounged around in their underwear.

Other early Munsingwear advertisements featured portraits of beautiful young maidens in their union suits, often modestly covered by a bouquet of flowers. With each passing year, the company grew bolder, removing flowers and showing more underwear and more skin. Underwear manufacturers such as Forest Mills and Avalon also advertised their union suits in magazines during this time period, but they used text to describe the underwear or showed images of their garments sans models. Ads for Lewis Union Suits depicted fully clothed women holding union suits.

Around the turn of the century, attitudes toward underwear were changing along with the nation's attitude toward health and exercise. Northwestern

Nicollet Avenue at Sixth Street South, Minneapolis, ca. 1900. These passers-by were a ready market for the company's products.

Ad, 1917. Munsingwear offered "athletic styles" in union suits for men at the height of the health and wellness trend that followed the Victorian era.

Ad, 1922. A popular theme in Munsingwear advertising of the decade: a gentleman of means, relaxing in his private quarters, wearing Munsingwear underwear

Knitting strategically aligned the Munsingwear suit as a "healthy" garment. The dress reform movement was sweeping the nation, brought on by healthful living enthusiasts and women's rights activists. Women were opting for clothes that wouldn't restrict, bunch, bind, or get in the way of movement as they increasingly participated in sports like bicycling and tennis. Shedding layers and pounds of Victorian-era undergarments, such as boned, lace-up corsets and layered petticoats, women opted instead for the physical and psychological freedom of less constricting underwear: bloomers, bandeaus (early brassieres), and other separates.

Men, on the other hand, didn't have as many restrictive undergarments to shed. (Although stomach-flattening corsets for men existed, they weren't common.)

Underwear manufacturers such as Munsingwear, B.V.D., and Glastenbury advertised their innerwear as "healthy" and "hygienic," with images of men in athletic pursuits wearing just their underwear. Munsingwear fully embraced the theme but also depicted the Munsingwear man as a gentleman of means, enjoying a reflective moment in his dressing quarters.

"The Largest Knitting Mill West of the Allegheny Mountains"

Production for the healthful Munsingwear union suit went into overdrive right before the turn of the century when the company expanded production to include an array of new styles. By the spring of 1900, Munsingwear offered sixty different union suits for women, ten for girls, four for boys, and six for men. According to a Munsingwear ad, "Whether you are tall or short, fat or thin, old or young, man, woman, boy or girl, there is a Munsingwear garment that will give you the utmost in service and satisfaction." As demand for union suits increased, Northwestern Knitting needed yet another home, a much larger one that could accommodate increased production.

Union suits grace the clothesline beneath the builders at 716–20 Glenwood Avenue in November 1914. The scaffolding outlines the water tower on what would become Building E, where bleaching, dyeing, fleecing, napping, cutting, sewing, and inspection took place.

Following numerous relocations around Minneapolis, the company started construction on a new underwear factory in 1904 on Minneapolis's north side. The new facility was actually five brick-and-concrete buildings that took up an entire square block that was bounded by Lyndale, Third, and Aldrich Avenues North and Glenwood Avenue.

The massive complex took eleven years to complete and was so large that it was common for new employees to get lost. Its 650,000 square feet contained almost six hundred knitting machines and sixteen hundred sewing machines for the production of cotton, worsted, and silk underwear, both knit and woven.

The company's building at 269–77 Lyndale Avenue housed the cafeteria as well as knitting, sewing, and pressing departments.

Employees pose in front of the Northwestern Knitting Company's new factory in an image that was replicated in newspapers around the nation, often with the caption, "Makers of Munsingwear at the Mammoth Modern Model Munsingwear Mills in Minneapolis," 1912.

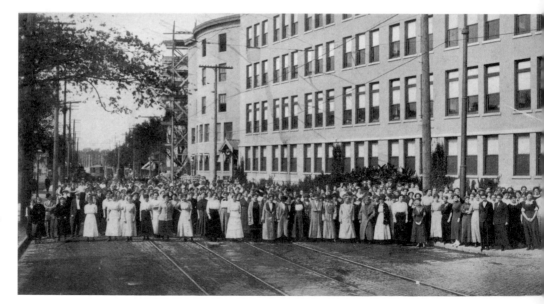

Northwestern Knitting touted its new home as "absolutely fireproof," clean, sanitary, well lit, and properly ventilated to bring health and vigor to the workers. The company also claimed that its workers, along "with the aid of ingenious machinery, are able to produce perfect fitting Munsingwear garments at a rate of 10,000 a day."

William C. Edgar, editor of Minnesota's premier literary magazine, *The Bellman,* wrote lovingly of his first visit to the three-acre factory: "Sheer wonder and amazement make one speechless as he is guided from floor to floor, and room to room through this enormous plant . . . Light, also, is everywhere. The windows are large, and even in the middle and the corners of the great rooms it is as bright as day." Edgar's first and last impression of Munsingwear was its "marvelous system of order" and exquisite cleanliness: "Everywhere the atmosphere is pure and clean, infinitely better than that to be found in ninety-nine out of a hundred of the business offices in the country."

The sprawling underwear factory and its steam whistle quickly became an integral part of the North Minneapolis community. The engineers took great pride in timing the noon blast to the exact second. The chief engineer stood with his hand on the whistle cord and his eye on the Western Union clock, waiting for

A bird's-eye view of the Munsingwear plant in North Minneapolis, ca. 1921. At its incorporation in 1923, Munsingwear was the largest worldwide manufacturer of underwear.

all the hands on the clock to line up perfectly on twelve, and when he yanked the cord, "the whistle would be heard all over Minneapolis." Nearby housewives knew their husbands would be coming home for lunch, and conductors on the streetcar line set their watches by the factory whistle.

The bronze, three-chambered steam whistle required a hundred pounds of steam for one ear-splitting blast. It was used for fifty years before the company switched to an electrically powered whistle. The retired steam whistle became a sundial in a Munsingwear vice president's garden before it was donated to the Minnesota Historical Society.

The Case of the Missing Underwear

Underwear thievery was a problem at the Northwestern Knitting Company—a problem the company would not tolerate. In 1915 Northwestern Knitting hired an undercover underwear detective from the legendary William J. Burns International Detective Agency to infiltrate an internal crime ring.

The underwear detective, Operative #71, disguised as a disgruntled laborer earning about $7.50 per week, sussed out the criminals and attempted to gain their trust. He soon found himself in the middle of a black market underwear operation in the stockroom. Operative #71 observed as several male employees wrapped union suits around their waists, sneaking them out for the purpose of selling them for $1.00 to $2.50. One of the detective's daily reports describes the criminal activity of an employee named Fritz:

> I saw when Fritz put the second suit of underwear around his belt. He told me that it was a good garment, and that some retailed for $39.00 per dozen. Fritz told me that this was the second pair of suits he had taken in the last four weeks, as he had become a little afraid, owing to Frank, the Superintendent, being around on the floor so much. Fritz said he did not give a "darn" for the plant, if it were not for these goods that he would get, which made up for the small pay he was getting. He further stated that he had played baseball for the Northwestern Knitting Mill all summer and never received a cent's reward, but all the players had been promised that they would be paid.

At the time, the union suits were packaged in boxes made right in the plant. The black market ring removed the suits and destroyed the boxes. Operative #71 found pieces of destroyed boxes and submitted them as evidence. The detective expanded the scope of the inquiry throughout the Twin Cities of Minneapolis and St. Paul by questioning former employees suspected of ties to the underwear black market. Operative #71 also tailed members of the ring to their rendezvous spot with buyers, noting packages exchanged hands.

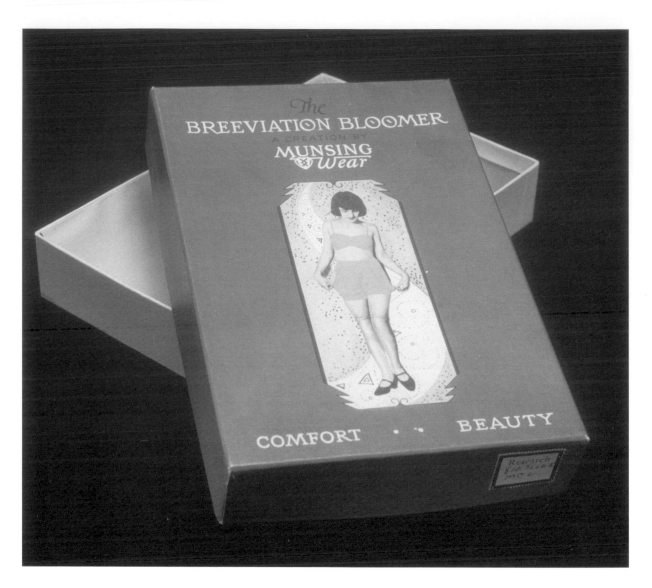

The
BREEVIATION BLOOMER
A CREATION BY
MUNSING Wear

COMFORT ∴ BEAUTY

Boxes for the undergarments were printed and assembled in the plant.

Each day the underwear detective submitted a report to the company, along with his daily expenses, which consisted of his bar tabs, meals, theater and baseball tickets, telephone calls, streetcar fare, and costs of bowling with the members of the crime ring. In the investigative process, Operative #71 detected more than just missing underwear. He also reported loafing, poor workflow, inefficiencies, and the names of female employees he suspected of trying to unionize for an eight-hour workday.

The underwear detective collected evidence, filed daily reports, and submitted a bill while investigating the black market underwear ring that operated inside the company.

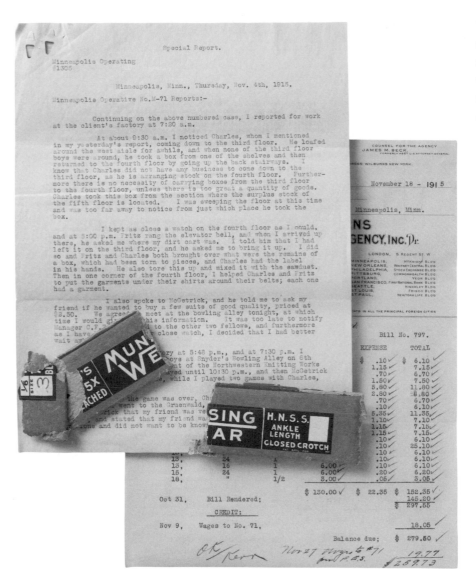

The employees suspected of unionizing were likely a greater threat to the company than the underwear thieves. At the time, Northwestern Knitting Company leaders, like so many Minneapolis businessmen, famously eschewed organized labor through the powerful Minneapolis Citizens Alliance—a group formed in opposition to unionization. The working class had very little influence over a company's desire to keep wages low and hours long for a healthy bottom line. The detective mentioned several times that employees were aware that informants worked among them, reporting on individuals suspected of anti-company behavior such as unionization.

Among the detective's most shocking findings was an employee with a raging case of gonorrhea and deplorable personal hygiene. Operative #71 advocated for the immediate dismissal of the man in question:

> This young man, Paul, I discovered today is affected by an objectionable disease, commonly known as gonorrhea and I have seen him at three different times in the toilet room medicating himself or otherwise using some cotton and some yellow powder with his bare hands, and then drying his hands on the towel without washing himself. These towels are used by other employees some of whom also dry their faces with them after washing.

The fate of "Gonorrhea Paul" is unknown, but after five weeks of investigation, arrests were made, confessions were signed, and jail time was served by those employees involved in the black market underwear ring at Northwestern Knitting Company. Operative #71 submitted his final bill, totaling $279.50.

3 MUNSINGITE

An underwear model,
1920s

BY 1917, Northwestern Knitting Mills was producing thirty thousand garments a day, due in no small part to a government contract to make long underwear for the U.S. troops serving in World War I. This high visibility for the Munsingwear brand gave the company widespread recognition, and to many people the brand became synonymous with quality underwear.

World War I fueled a pro-America sentiment that ran deep in the Midwest. It also permitted the persecution of German Americans and the deliberate repression of labor and radical groups seeking reforms. At the Northwestern Knitting Company, patriotism coupled with paternalistic expectations resulted in a widely successful war effort. Many male employees enlisted, and the newsletter published letters they wrote back to the company. Employees worked long shifts for war production; a 1919 newsletter included a photo of company trucks that "helped to 'Make the Hun Hunt His Hole,'" with one of them carrying a record 10,400 pounds of underwear in one day for "Uncle Sam Fighters."

All female employees—wholesome, selfless women—were strongly encouraged to "take up their share in War Relief Work" by volunteering for the in-house Red Cross Surgical Dressing Unit. For women working fifty-four hours and earning up to $40.00 per week, these additional hours were no small sacrifice. Approximately four hundred women donned nurses' uniforms, rolled up their sleeves, and made surgical dressings in the after-hours war effort. The company's newsletter praised them in the January 1919 issue: "This has been a wonderful time for these women to show their true value. Patriotism is not all, it is the giving of one's self to something really worthwhile. No doubt there is

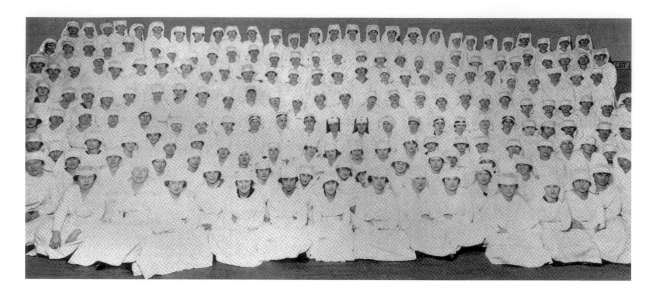

The American Red Cross Surgical Dressing Unit of the Northwestern Knitting Company in 1919. The women volunteered, after work hours, to knit, sew, cut, and package various surgical-related dressing to aid in the war effort.

not the slightest shadow of regret on the part of any young woman in the whole plant because of what she has done for the Red Cross, but there is without a doubt, a great rejoicing in the heart of each member over the fact that she had a part in making the world a place of usefulness and unselfish devotion."

In 1919 alone, the Northwestern Knitting Company reported manufacturing over 82,000 compresses, cotton surgical pads, sponges, oakum pads, wipes, one-inch packings, and face masks. Civic and government leaders applauded the company and its employees for their exemplary contributions to war relief work.

After World War I, George Munsing rejoined the company following a sabbatical of twenty-four years. Munsing left in 1895 to pursue a career as an inventor. Upon his return, he took a position as a "research investigator" and was honored by the company he started when the name was changed to the Munsingwear Company. Subsequently, company officials started to fondly refer to all employees as "Munsingites." A company booklet published in 1921, *The Success of Well Doing,* presented a glowing vision of postwar cooperation: "Munsingites are 100% Americans. Their names may be Olsen or Nelson, O'Brien or McCarthy, Schumacher or Schneider, Baker or Brewer, MacTavish, La Pierre, or Pulaski, but they are all Americans—because they love America; because this is their country; because their lives are bound up in the destinies of this nation."

At this time, Munsingwear was Minnesota's largest employer of women. Of its more than three thousand workers, 85 percent were women, many of whom were immigrants. Up to twenty different nationalities (all Caucasian) were represented at the company, and many languages were spoken throughout the factory. However, English was always encouraged.

Munsingwear offered free Americanization night classes for its new immigrant employees for the "purpose of becoming better Americans." Munsingite Hulda Koskie won first prize for her essay, "Why Do I Like My School?" in which she wrote, "I like my school for the reason that there I will learn the English language, which is my greatest ambition, although it seems very hard to learn and understand. But the school in itself is so interesting that one forgets little hardships. In our class this term we have such a kind and lovable teacher that it would seem a crime to miss one evening of school."

Besides the English language, new immigrants studied math, geography, history, government, physiology, and "other subjects which every good American should know." United States citizenship classes were also offered.

For all the education opportunities at Munsingwear, American-born employees received preferential treatment in the division of labor. Almost all supervisors were American born. Certain immigrant groups, such as Swedish, Norwegian, Finnish, and German, fared well in the coveted positions of packaging and inspection. Employees in these positions were not paid by the piece but rather received a set wage. Other immigrants, Polish and Russian women, for example, were often relegated to tedious and labor-intensive tasks. Certainly there were exceptions, but overall, American-born Munsingites enjoyed the greatest benefits.

Munsingwear's publicity materials and company histories put the sordid past of lunch-stealing management and unfair labor practices far behind it, stating, "The workers, as individuals, produce 'quality' work only when they work in cooperative harmony under wholesome and happy surroundings." Opportunities awaited all workers who had "that greatest of all qualifications— plain, every-day common sense." Persons thus equipped were sure to strive for good health, neat appearance, and a "wholesome enthusiasm for work." Anyone seeking employment would be welcome and "extended every courtesy" as they waited to be interviewed.

William Edgar described the typical female Munsingite: "Eyes are bright and clear, cheeks are rosy, fingers are fresh and active . . . The women and girls who make Munsingwear are as neatly and as well, yes, as fashionably dressed as their sisters who may be found shopping on the retail streets."

The company's appealing images of the life of a Munsingite do not mention the danger of the work. Evelina Johansdotter, a Swedish immigrant to Minnesota, wrote of her experience working on the Munsingwear sewing machines: "Only once did I sew over my fingers so that the needle broke into several pieces. I stayed calm however, quickly wrapping my finger tightly in a handkerchief, put in a new needle, and continued sewing as if nothing had happened. It was not until lunch break that I could examine my finger—luckily I discovered no pieces of needle in my finger, but it was seriously injured."

Other Munsingites weren't as lucky, passing out when the needle punctured their skin and broke off in their hands, requiring a doctor to remove the bits of broken needle. "It was quite common," noted Johansdotter, "that especially the beginners sewed over their fingers . . . very likely because of the speed of the machines which were electrically powered."

Some of what Munsingwear provided at this time was truly progressive. To give Munsingites the medical attention they needed, Munsingwear's medical department consisted of an in-house nurse and others who made regular visits: general practitioners, an otolaryngologist (ear, nose, and throat specialist), a dental assistant, and a dentist. Medical services were free to all employees, which was likely crucial considering the purity of the air was undoubtedly exaggerated and most employees were handling sharp, machine-powered needles on a daily basis.

Through the medical department, the company continuously promoted health and happiness as the virtues of efficient work: "Health and happiness become a contagion which permeates every department so that, as one large

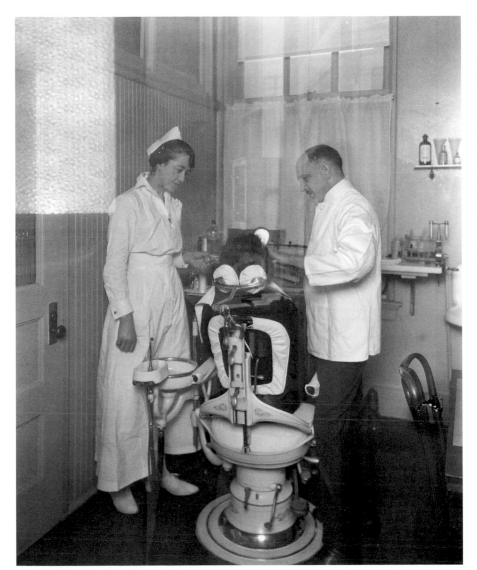

Dentist Dr. Mieson with a dental hygienist and patient in the company's on-site dental office, 1920. The company also had a general physician, nurses, and an ears, nose, and throat (ENT) specialist on staff. Employees received free dental and medical care and were eligible for health insurance through the company if their medical needs exceeded an average office visit.

family, Munsingites work in an atmosphere that makes for efficiency, good will and contentment." The company acknowledged that their workers could not possibly feel the certain joy in performing their task when they were suffering from ill health: "Our Medical Department . . . is here to serve our workers, not in any patronizing way, but in the best of spirit and for the good of all."

An employee who missed work due to illness could count on "a friendly visitor"—Mrs. Katherine A. Ellis—who checked on the validity of the illness and offered assistance. This policy was presented as a service to employees in need, but it must also have worked to discourage faked illnesses:

> It is so comforting to receive a friendly visit from this motherly woman. If something more than just a friendly call is needed, Mrs. Ellis renders service in the same friendly way and to such extent as the occasion requires. Surprising, as it may seem, in the past year Mrs. Ellis made over eighteen hundred calls on members of the Munsingwear family. A visitor with pleasing personality certainly has power to infuse hope and cheer into the sickroom. This hastens the recovery of the patient, as recovery is bound to be retarded where a patient must suffer alone and unfriended.

If a Munsingite felt unwell at work but not sick enough to go home, there was a resting room: a large room next to the recreation room furnished with beds, pillows, and warm blankets: "Any girl who is ill or in any way indisposed finds this room open to her. Very often a complete relaxation for a half hour or more if necessary, will prove so beneficial that a girl is able to go back to work refreshed in mind and body." Presumably, male employees were left to their own devices, either to tough it out all day when they didn't feel well or to head home to await their visit from Mrs. Ellis.

Many of the women working for Munsingwear were a part of the boardinghouse migration—a large community of young women who left their rural roots seeking employment in large, urban centers. Boardinghouses were teeming with new urbanites and new immigrants, all eager to find a network of friends, meet eligible young men, and create new families. Some women were there out of choice, while others were forced to leave the farm, to lessen the burden on their families.

Munsingwear created a social service department to help its employees' transition to Minneapolis. A homelike recreation room was established where workers could gather to read, sew, socialize, play the piano, sing, and dance. The company promoted the room's use to employees, saying "because the room is

so very spacious no end of fun and frolic can be had. Entertainments, such as musical comedies, home talent plays, and so forth, are also held here."

A staff member who acted as a housemother was on duty to be a "friend and friendly advisor to all who come to her." To keep its workforce viable, Munsingwear management ensured that its employees had stable and safe living arrangements and an easy way in which they could connect with their sisters in the needle trade: "There is a feeling of security to the strange or homesick girl, when she learns that she need not be utterly friendless because she happens to be here alone in a strange city."

Social activities at Munsingwear were bountiful and well attended because the majority of staff were young and unmarried. The Munsingwear Music Club, in particular, was a big hit among Munsingites. All employees were welcome to join and perform in their singing society, orchestra, musicals, and vaudeville

An impressive, fully staffed kitchen served the company's thousands of employees, who took their lunches in shifts.

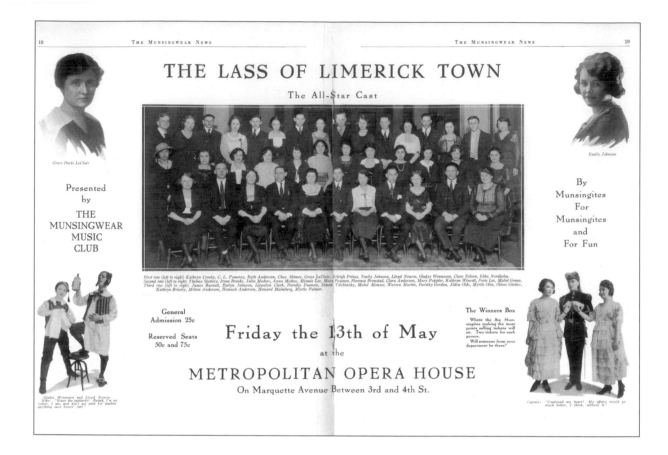

18   THE MUNSINGWEAR NEWS   THE MUNSINGWEAR NEWS   19

THE LASS OF LIMERICK TOWN

The All-Star Cast

Grace Davis LeClair

Emily Johnson

Presented
by
THE
MUNSINGWEAR
MUSIC
CLUB

By
Munsingites
For
Munsingites
and
For Fun

First row (left to right) Kathryn Crosby, C. L. Pomeroy, Ruth Anderson, Chas. Shimer, Grace LeClair, Arleigh Prince, Emily Johnson, Lloyd Nourse, Gladys Wenneson, Clara Nelson, Ebba Nordholm.
Second row (left to right) Thelma Slattery, Irene Brooks, Julia Meduc, Anna Meduc, Minnie Lee, Mary Posmer, Florence Bronstad, Clara Anderson, Mary Poppler, Kathryn Wincott, Josie Lee, Mabel Gonea.
Third row (left to right) James Burnett, Evelyn Johnson, Llewelyn Clark, Dorothy Duemoe, Simon Tolchinsky, Mabel Monson, Warren Martin, Dorothy Gordon, Alden Olds, Myrtle Olin, Oliver Giebler, Kathryn Briarly, Milton Anderson, Hannah Anderson, Howard Malmberg, Myrtle Palmer.

General
Admission 25c

Reserved Seats
50c and 75c

The Winners Box

Where the Six Mun-
singites making the most
points selling tickets will
sit. Two tickets for each
person.
Will someone from your
department be there?

Friday the 13th of May

at the

METROPOLITAN OPERA HOUSE

On Marquette Avenue Between 3rd and 4th St.

*Gladys Wenneson and Lloyd Nourse.
Mike: "Rinse the tankards! Bested, I'm an
'ostler, I am, and don't get paid for 'mashin'
anything save honest 'ale."*

*Captain: "Confound my heart! My affairs would go
much better, I think, without it."*

The company newsletter promoted the staff musical for 1921.

acts. The Munsingwear Orchestra performed every Thursday during the lunch break. And the musicals were so popular that they were held off-site, in theaters like the Metropolitan Opera House in Minneapolis that could accommodate large audiences.

The company encouraged comradely and good, clean, sweaty fun through Munsingwear-sponsored team sports such as kittenball, basketball, baseball, and bowling. Munsingwear even had an on-site gymnasium. Employee sports teams were always segregated by gender: "girls'" and "men's." In the 1920s, the Girls' Kitten Ball Club was among the most competitive, often winning community and city league championships. The Men's Inter-house Kitten Ball League was composed of six teams that played one another. Scores, stats, and game commentary were often published in the company newsletter. These

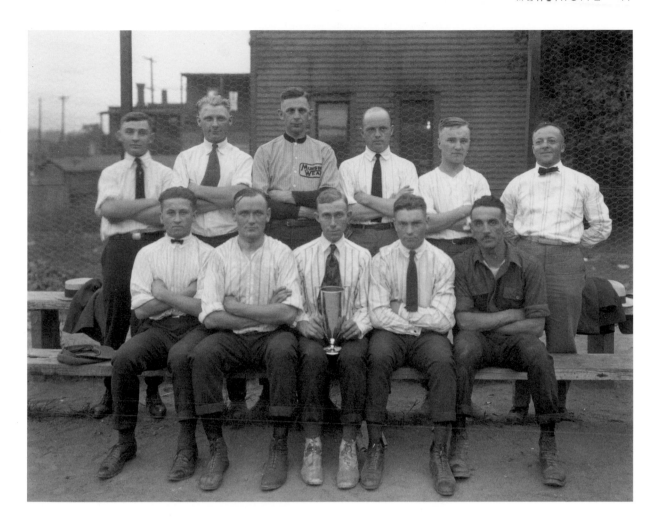

sports clubs and teams were either free to employees or available for a nominal fee. According to the company, "We are proud of the Munsingites who represent us in the field of sports. They keep in mind, in play as well as in work, the ideal of teamwork, fair play and true sportsmanship."

Munsingwear held many companywide events outside the factory walls, including an annual summer picnic, county fairs, concerts, sporting events, dances, and Christmas parties. Families of Munsingites were invited to attend many of these events, and the press often tagged along and reported about Munsingwear's social activities. On July 22, 1916, the *Minneapolis Journal* reported, "Some 1,900 sisters in the Mun Sin Wear sorority picnicked at Spring

Munsingwear's men's baseball team, pictured here in the summer of 1920 with trophy, played other company teams throughout the Twin Cities in a championship league.

The Munsingwear Kittens, from an issue of *Munsingwear News*, 1921, played kittenball, a precursor of softball. Munsingwear sports teams played in community intramural leagues and were known as serious competitors throughout the Twin Cities. The company's "girls'" kittenball and basketball teams often held championship titles.

Park, Lake Minnetonka, all day yesterday. Miles away from their knitting and tending to everything else but that, the girls ran races, played ball, swam, listened to a hired soldier band, danced to the music of a hired orchestra, lunched under the trees near the water's edge . . . Of course there were men at the picnic, but they were truly inconsiderable."

Total attendance at the event was three thousand—the largest outing ever for a Minneapolis company. Prizes for the potato sack and three-legged races and for the games of leapfrog and tug-of-war included chocolates, cuff links, and company underwear and silk stockings.

That particular annual picnic fell on the birthday of Munsingwear vice president E. J. Couper. The *Minneapolis Tribune* reported that a birthday cake weighing thirty-two pounds and measuring eighteen inches high and twenty-two inches square had been prepared by the Munsingite chef, C. W. Schlegel: "The cake was served by Mrs. Couper, her nephew and her daughters, to all comers. And they came, too, by the hundreds. It lasted about an hour until only small boys sidled up to the table to glean the last bit of frosting."

Munsingwear News

The company's exhaustive newsletter, "our internal house organ, *The Munsingwear News*," was a monthly, illustrated publication "for no other purpose than to serve Munsingites, to acquaint them with each other and with the Company and to add human interest to their work."

Each department had reporters who wrote about the activities both in and out of work. Birth announcements, wedding photos, recipes, poems, photo contests, jokes, gossip, and idle chatter commonly made it into the pages of the *Munsingwear News*.

In the issue for April 1920, for example, Department J—a light-weight finishing department—teased one of their own about a secret she had yet to share: "Why has Janette Jellivm been having such a big smile on her face lately? Tell us about it, Janette, you might as well now as later." Whether it was a new beau, engagement, or pregnancy, Department J doesn't say, but it did report, "Edith Solsvig Bolstad, the prominent soloist of Munsingwear, left on February 28th. Her girl friends presented her with a beautiful bouquet of jonquils on the last day when she played and sang for us in the recreation room. The girls all miss her very much. Edith is going to start housekeeping in May. She and her

A SERIES OF WORKPLACE
SCENES, 1920S

Munsingites wind yarn
and thread onto spools in
Department A, the winding
department. Each woman
watched about twenty
bobbins and tied yarn that
broke.

husband will make their home here in the city near Glenwood Lake. Good luck to Edith is the wish from our girls."

Department H, where heavy-weight fabrics were finished—reported the illnesses of department employees and the return of Adele Gustofson's purse, which had between twelve and fifteen dollars in it, along with photos of downtown Minneapolis. Gustofson awarded the finder of the purse five dollars.

Department H also reported, "Surprise! Who said girls couldn't keep a secret? Leave it to the girls of Department H. A real surprise party was given in honor of Hazel Olsen at her home, the night of her birthday, February 26. The evening was spent in singing, dancing and playing games, after which a buffet was served . . . All declared having the time of their life and were reluctant to leave."

Each publication of *Munsingwear News* was centered on a theme such as

The spools of yarn were placed on the knitting machine's spindles and threaded into the machine's needle. A Munsingite attends a knitting machine in the 1920s.

health, continuing education, volunteering, socializing, personal hygiene, exercise, or self-improvement. Tips for thrift—for instance, "Let's make it our new year's resolution to spend less than we earn!"—were sprinkled throughout the January 1920 issue.

Women at knitting machines, 1920. Each worker handled several machines, tying yarns when they broke and calling an adjuster if repairs were needed. There were different rooms for light-weight and medium-weight knitting.

Through the *Munsingwear News,* the company encouraged employees to go to church, live near the factory, enjoy music, and even garden in their spare time: "A great many of our Munsingwear family have cultivated gardens at home in the past few years and appreciate the enjoyment there is to be had in working in the garden a little each evening and watching the results."

If Munsingites didn't have their own yards to garden, the company offered a solution. In cooperation with the Minneapolis Garden Club, Munsingwear purchased garden plots for employees to cultivate for just two dollars a season. Seeds and flower bulbs were free to employees.

More than anything, the company promoted reading among employees. As early as 1911, it coordinated with Gratia Countryman, director of the Minneapolis Public Library (and pioneer of the bookmobile), to establish a library branch

in the factory. In a *Munsingwear News* issue devoted to reading, the company extolled learning and self-improvement:

> It's up to you to be alert, progressive, and up-to-date! You can be if you read one good book and a few magazine articles a month. Get them at the Munsingwear Library!
>
> Why let your education stop? Read on the street car on the way to work, read to children, read while waiting for a meal at a restaurant, read plays, poetry or fiction on cold winter evenings, memorize poetry, and read while getting your hair cut instead of listening to beauty shop gossip.

The branch evolved into a busy library, run by Munsingwear's social service

The bleaching department, around 1920, where woven cotton fabrics were boiled, washed, and bleached in immense kettles about seven feet in diameter and seven feet deep, then rinsed and dried. The department was staffed exclusively by men who were rumored to strip down to less than their union suits to survive the heat.

In the brushing department, the knitted material went through a fleecing or napping operation to raise the fabric, giving it a "fluffy feel." Because the work required lifting heavy spools of fabric, this department employed only men.

department for the purpose of helping employees to grow professionally and personally. In this era just before radios became widespread, evenings could be a little dull, and Munsingwear didn't want its employees to turn to vices: "There are times, when night comes, when our brains cease to function properly, and when we yearn for a book of good fiction, rich with pulsations of life, color and realistic human drama. This change of scene and surrounding does much to rest and fit us for tomorrow."

By 1920, the library program was circulating seventy-five hundred books and innumerable pamphlets. Munsingwear's plan to get employees reading was working.

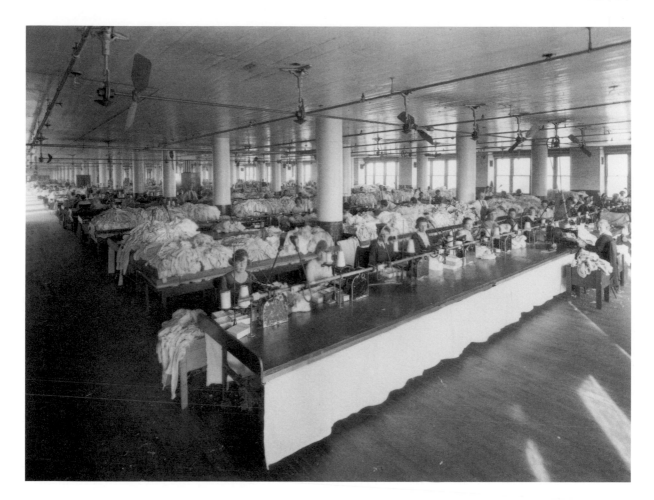

In the April 1920 issue of *Munsingwear News*, the company printed an article about suffrage. This topic was especially timely, considering that most of the employees at Munsingwear were women and they didn't yet have the right to vote in political elections. It mused, "Will woman suffrage merely increase the number of ballots cast, leaving the final results unchanged? Or will the entry of women into politics exert a purifying influence? . . . Women undoubtedly will be able to improve politics if large numbers of them seriously undertake the task. A certain type [of] woman, the kind that seeks only selfish ends, will exert an evil influence upon politics. But happily these women are the exception."

The article implied that any woman reading a Munsingwear newsletter was not the kind of woman who would "exert an evil influence." Instead, she was

By the 1920s, Munsingwear was manufacturing thirty thousand undergarments a day. Each garment worker in the several finishing work rooms was expected to sew hundreds of garments each day. The constant whir from the machines would have been deafening. At the end of the process, noted the company's literature, "The garment is on its way rejoicing to the next stage of its completion."

After garments were inspected, the pressing department took over, preparing garments for boxing.

made of the high moral fiber that would improve politics. Perhaps, too, the article served as subtle warning to female employees not to abuse the power of the vote should it be granted to them, nor to get drunk on power and advocate for an eight-hour workday. A few months later, the Nineteenth Amendment, which granted women the right to vote, was finally ratified by the state of Tennessee and passed into federal law.

Munsingwear's management style solved many problems for employees, and employees thus supported would not have to make important decisions on their own, especially political decisions that might interfere with the company's best interests. Still, many employees found the careers they were looking for at Munsingwear. Some women spent their entire work lives with the company,

Munsingwear printed all its own sales material, retail store literature, and garment boxes. Printshop employees pose in 1920 in one of the company's only truly mixed-gender departments.

rising from the ranks of machine operators to garment inspectors and on to supervisors. And male employees could, of course, go farther, catapulting from "general utility boy" or shipping clerk to company patent holder and officer. F. M. Sowell, for example, was hired as a shipping clerk and rose to be president, serving from 1913 to 1932. Another employee, Franklin Chatfield, was hired in 1902 to repair and maintain machinery and went on to hold thirty-four patents, sixteen of which were on garments and eighteen on machines. By the time Chatfield retired in 1950, he played a role in developing 133 Munsingwear patents.

In a regular feature of *Munsingwear News* called "Why I Like to Be a Munsingite," employees wrote about their contentment with working for the company. The reasons ranged from an appreciation for the open workspaces and never having to worry about a fire breaking out to all the social activities available, getting time off when needed, and the opportunity to take English classes at work, free of charge.

The company used fitting models to show off its newest offerings, probably in the early 1920s; the resulting images could be redrawn as advertisements.

Munsingwear's management didn't hide the fact that it was a paternalistic company, but it also went to great lengths to provide employees with benefits that workers at other factories did not enjoy. The company was also committed to cultivating employees and promoting talent from within. Internal publications like *The Success of Well Doing* and the *Munsingwear News* painted the company in an impossibly radiant light, particularly for modern readers, but in reality Munsingwear was a respectable place to work with exceptional benefits and countless opportunities for an enriching after-hours life.

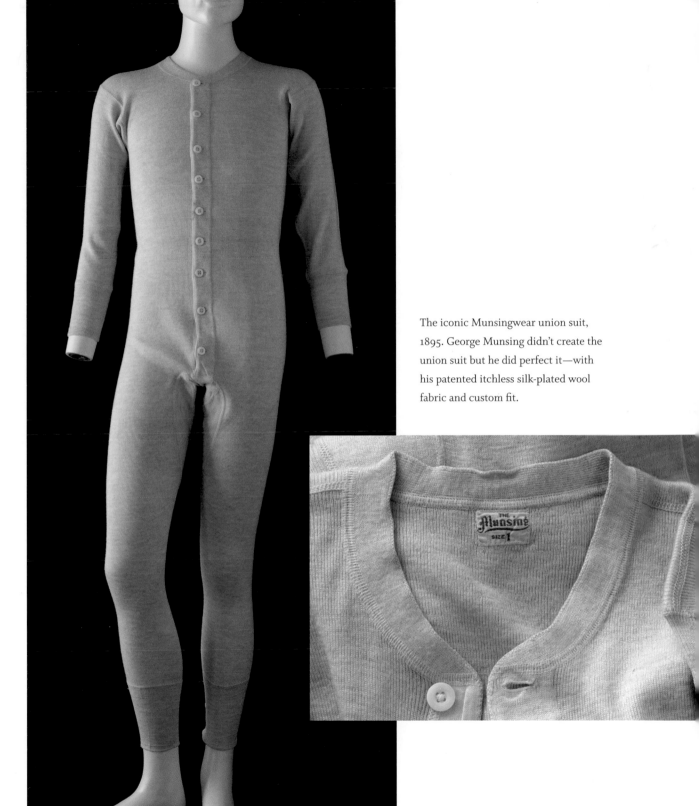

The iconic Munsingwear union suit, 1895. George Munsing didn't create the union suit but he did perfect it—with his patented itchless silk-plated wool fabric and custom fit.

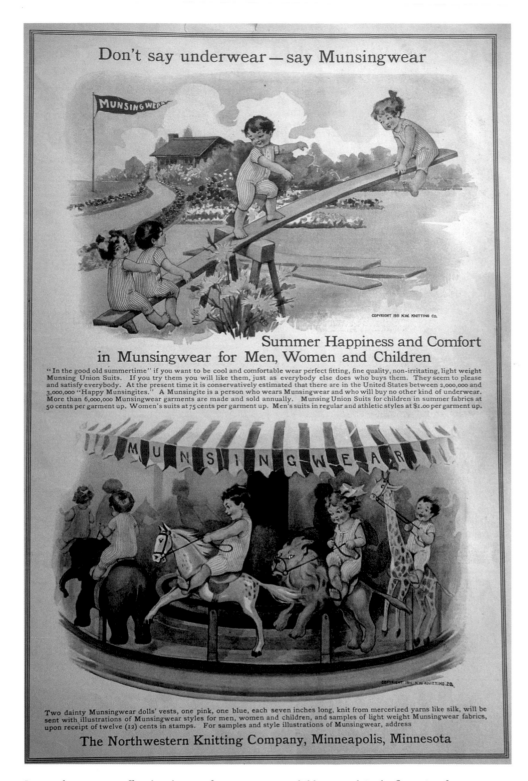

In 1911 the company offered underwear for men, women, children—and, in the fine print, for even smaller customers. "Two dainty Munsingwear dolls' vests, one pink, one blue" were available for discerning dolls everywhere.

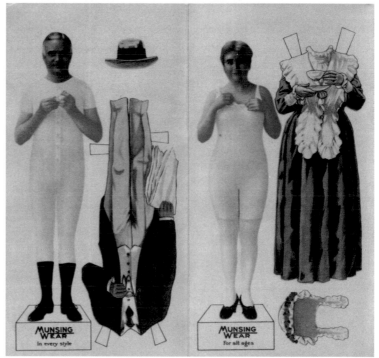

Another giveaway "beyond compare": a paper doll Munsingwear family, about 1917

56

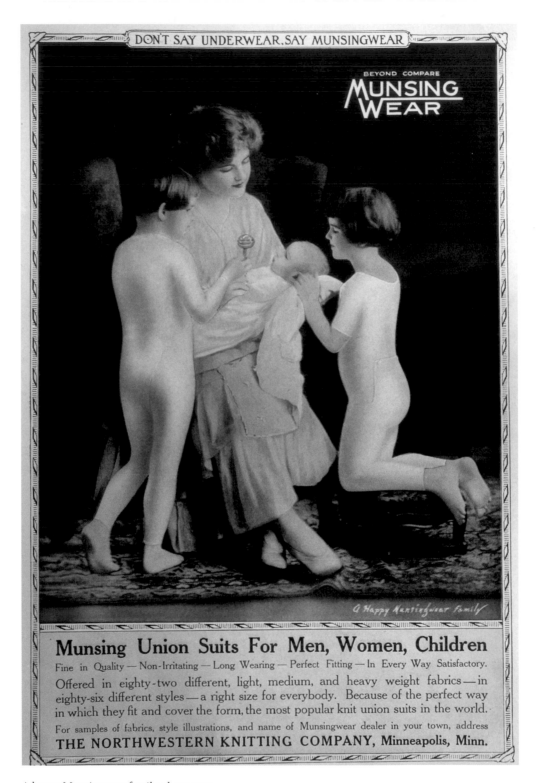

A happy Munsingwear family, about 1915

As Munsingwear's underwear offerings expanded in the 1920s, advertisements began to show a broader range of garments.

MUNSING Wear *presents* Foundettes

Munsingwear makes all styles of smart undergarments in all types of fabrics. For men, women and children.
UNDERWEAR · WATERWEAR · HOSIERY
SLEEPING AND LOUNGING GARMENTS · KNIT COATS
PULL-ONS · FOUNDATION GARMENTS

Brand New Foundation Garments of a Brand New Fabric, Invented by MUNSINGWEAR

YOU'VE never seen step-in girdles and foundation garments quite like these . . . for nothing like them has ever been created! Foundettes slim the hips, trim the waist, flatten the diaphragm and smooth the silhouette into smart and lovely lines. Yet, you've never worn anything quite so comfortable! Fashioned of specially processed two-way-stretch fabric . . . invented by Munsingwear . . . Foundettes will wash marvelously and wear wonderfully. They won't pull away from the seams or ravel back or curl. You'll like Munsingwear Foundettes for slimmer figures. And they're priced for slimmer purses. See these new Foundettes at a Munsingwear dealer near you. Munsingwear, Minneapolis.

LET MUNSINGWEAR COVER YOU WITH SATISFACTION

In the 1930s designer Ruth Kapinas experimented with Lastex, a new elasticized yarn, to create the Foundettes line, Munsingwear's most popular foundation undergarment. By 1933, Foundettes were trimming women's figures with "two-way-stretch fabric."

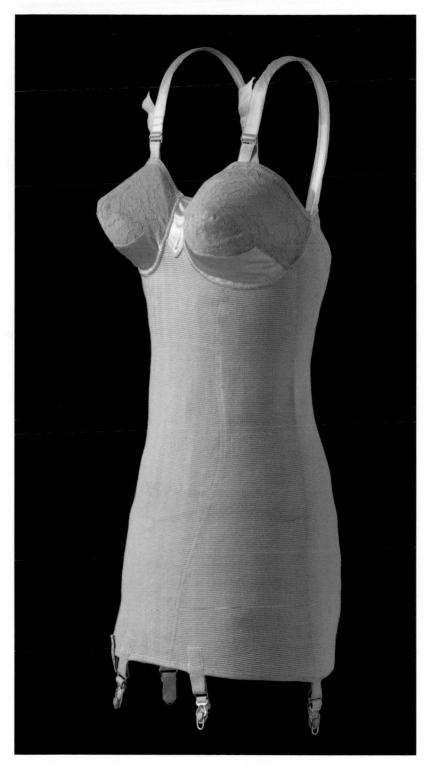

This cotton stars-and-stripes set, never sold, was used in a store display to show Munsingwear's support of the United States during World War II.

New..

STYLE-KNITTED

SKIN-FITTED

Ponies *by*

MUNSING *Wear*

Light-weight yet warm. And very smart! And how smooth they fit beneath smooth frocks!

UNDIES must fit to perfection . . . the new tight-fitting clothes demand it! They must wear and wash and live a long and lovely life. Trim little, slim little Munsingwear "Ponies".... knit panties and vests.... are styled for slim modern dresses and priced for thin modern budgets. Snug and warm for winter winds, in specially processed Munsingwear Rayon, in Silk, in Rayon-and-Cotton, and in Worsted-Cotton-and-Rayon. In a good store nearby. Munsingwear, Minneapolis.

Munsingwear makes all styles of smart undergarments in all types of fabrics. For men, women and children.

UNDERWEAR · WATERWEAR
SLEEPING AND LOUNGING GARMENTS
HOSIERY · KNIT COATS · PULL-ONS
FOUNDATION GARMENTS

LET MUNSINGWEAR COVER YOU WITH SATISFACTION

Ponies, lightweight and warm, were introduced in the late 1930s and by the early 1940s were helping women ready themselves for war work.

The 1950s silhouette was popularized by Hollywood Vassarette's heavily stitched whirlpool bra, also known as the bullet or torpedo bra. The fabric of choice for bras and panties in the postwar era was nylon.

From functional to fabulous: a Hollywood Vassarette girdle (below) and merry widow of the 1960s

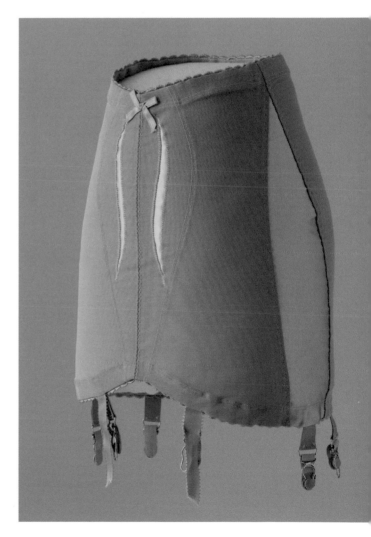

Vassarette was an industry leader in the marketing of dainty lace-embellished undergarments like this slip, 1960s.

The Caprice de Coeur peignoir and gown set from Hollywood Vassarette's 1964 designer line

COLORS GO MAD

and you'll feel so glad in new "Flowers Flambeau" print! It sends sparks of color excitement throughout your fall wardrobe...smoulders under the season's important reds, blazes beneath its ultra blues, kindles young sophistication under black or greys. In this anything-goes fashion mood, "Flowers Flambeau" nylon bra, 5.00; nylon petticoat, 5.95; long-leg pantie, 10.00. At the fine fashion stores that are upsetting the color cart this fall...underneath-it-all!

HOLLYWOOD *Vassarette* BRAS GIRDLES LINGERIE
DIV. OF MUNSINGWEAR, INC. • 261 MADISON AVE., NEW YORK CITY

For: ✱ FRENCH VOGUE — September 1963
✱ FRENCH HAUTE COUTURE — September 1963
✱ VOGUE — September 15, 1963
✱ BRITISH HARPERS BAZAAR — September 1963

The Colors Go Mad line was a fully coordinated set designed by Jean Norman Hall in 1963.

Hollywood Vassarette's 1961 offerings included a coordinated undergarment line in Toulouse print.

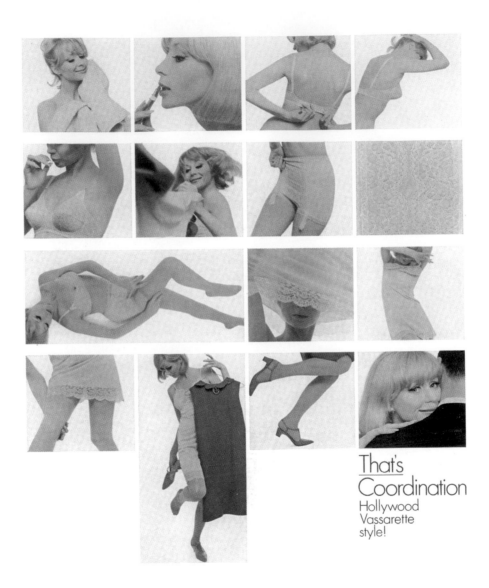

That's
Coordination
Hollywood
Vassarette
style!

From the inside out, and to the tips of your toes, Hollywood Vassarette coordinates you in Amber Gold...rich new color underneath-it-all!
Whirlpool® bra, personally fitted $4, matchmaker leg panty $8, and lacy slip in junior or misses sizes $6, to gold textured HV stockings $2.

HOLLYWOOD VASSARETTE® BRAS, GIRDLES, MISSES AND JUNIOR LINGERIE, STOCKINGS / DIV. OF MUNSINGWEAR INC., 261 MADISON AVE., NEW YORK CITY

A thoroughly coordinated woman's dressing process becomes a visual dance, as advertised in *Mademoiselle* in 1965.

Munsingwear models,
early 1920s

4 In the Mood for Munsingwear

Ad, *Fruit, Garden and Home* magazine, 1923. This ad captures a transitional moment in Munsingwear's history. The company was adding new lines of intimate apparel to its standard union suits.

AT THE END of an immensely lucrative decade, the Munsingwear Company went public in 1923, becoming the Munsingwear Corporation. The budding underwear empire became the largest manufacturer in the world producing underwear under one trademark, with an ever-increasing array of garments for men, women, children, and infants. An ad from 1923 that ran in *Fruit, Garden and Home* magazine features various Munsingwear underwear styles and fabrics for babies, girls, and women, with this accompanying copy: "The woven garments may be had in white and pastel shades in voiles, mulls, crepes and tub silks in dainty feminine suits for women and a great variety of light weight fabrics in athletic styles for men."

The need for union suits was waning, though, thanks to improvements in household heating and dramatic changes in fashion and lifestyle that made the beloved union suit nearly obsolete. Flappers, with their short skirts and drop waists, wanted nothing to do with grandma's union suit, whether it itched or not, opting instead for loose-fitting bloomers, one-piece slips, chemises, and camisoles.

Certainly flappers represented only a fraction of women in the 1920s, yet styles were undoubtedly changing across America. Women were wearing fewer layers, shorter hemlines, lighter fabrics, and more silk stockings. Men's clothing was becoming less bulky, less complicated, and less layered as well. Sweeping changes in the nation's fashions meant that Munsingwear had to keep up, and in so doing, the company helped to change America's underwear.

Design

Around 1920, Munsingwear became one of the first apparel companies to establish a design department, headed by clothing designer Beulah Spilsbury, formerly of Columbia University in New York. Spilsbury helped the company venture into new territory with modern styles and fabrics. Without completely eliminating traditional underwear offerings, Munsingwear expanded its line to include lingerie, sleepwear (often referred to as "nightwear"), hosiery, coats, "waterwear," and loungewear.

Underwear styles were easy to predict prior to World War I, noted Munsingwear's sales material, but afterward, it was a different story:

> Now it is essential to keep ahead of the style and color trend, and to this end our Designing Department functions.
>
> By keeping in constant touch with the developments in Paris and New York, particularly as regards fashions in outer dress, our designers are able to forecast new underwear requirements and to create new designs to meet the mode. Garments are always modeled on live figures, and each proposed change, or new style, is given thorough wearing and washing tests to determine its practicability before being adopted for the Munsingwear line.

The design department captured the impetuous, youthful spirit of the 1920s with a fully illustrated sales brochure, *The Curtain Rises on Munsingwear Modes.* Young, glamorous models posed in various ensembles, like the Modernistic Wrap, a balloon motif robe; the Sorority Jacket, a sleek loungewear cover-up; and the body-conscious Shadow Skirt, a rayon slip with shading that was "cleverly designed to enhance the straight-line silhouette of the season" under the flimsiest of skirts and dresses.

Rayon, a semi-synthetic fiber neither completely synthetic nor completely natural, was developed in Europe and quickly became a favorite of garment manufacturers around the globe. By mixing organic solvents with the nitrocellulose from wood pulp, chemists could create artificial silk. DuPont,

PRESENTING . . . . THE PANTIE CHEMISE
with Leg Band in Contrasting Color

A flippant little garment, this . . . just waiting to go a-dancing 'neath a picturesque frock. A mere handful of gleaming Munsingwear Rayon, yet durable, too. Bodice top with drawstring band. Semi-fitted legs held snugly by snap fasteners and banded with a gay, contrasting color. Available in the most popular colors, in sizes for all figures. Model 163.

MUNSING

MODERNISTIC WRAP

L'Art Moderne has inspired this dashing Robe for the modern maid and matron. Flashing balloon-design applique . . . alluringly feminine lines. Of clear, shimmering Munsingwear Rayon in several smart color combinations. All sizes. Model 205.

MUNSING

As union suits fell out of fashion, Munsingwear established a design department that helped expand the company's offerings to include lingerie— where function played second to fashion. These pages from *The Curtain Rises on Munsingwear Modes*, 1920, show off the new offerings.

PATTERNED SHORTS

Daringly boyish, yet fitting the feminine figure exactly . . . these frivolous Shorts boast a yoke front, button at left hip. Uplift Bandeau to match. In many smart patterns all sizes. Shorts—Model 998; Bandeau—Model 970.

MUNSING

RAYON SHORTS

The younger set will adore Shorts of White Munsingwear Rayon with a contrasting stripe . . . flat yoke front and removable elastic across the back. Bandeau, plain or trimmed in black, flame or turquoise to match. All sizes. Bandeau — Model 330; Shorts—Model 360.

MUNSING

the American chemical company, began to sell short-stranded fiber in bulk to garment manufacturers like Munsingwear for the mass production of rayon and rayon-blend garments that were cheaper and more plentiful than silk.

Ad, 1937. Munsingwear never shied away from male bonding themes in its ads, especially ones that featured sports and the beauty of the male form.

THEY FEEL RIGHT—A WELL-BALANCED RACQUET AND THIS WELL-CUT *Skit-Suit*

HERE'S cool comfort and body ease you've never had before. SKIT-Suits by Munsingwear that look like shirts and shorts—so brief you don't know you're wearing them—so expertly cut and tailored they can't bag or bunch. And note the three special comfort features... no-gap buttonless fly... elastic leg-openings and waist band... full seat coverage with elastic drop seat. Treat yourself to perfect comfort with SKIT-Suits. Also "by Munsingwear" is a complete line for men ... SKIT-Shorts, fancy shorts, knit underwear of every type as well as smart sox. Treat yourself to comfort and quality by asking for "Munsingwear." At quality stores. MUNSINGWEAR, Minneapolis.

Munsingwear's bloomers, shorts, panties, knickers, drawers, "stepins," and "pullons"—women's underpants—came in all sizes, styles, and colors in the 1920s. The company also introduced "bandeaus" and "uplift bandeaus," early versions of brassieres that were like tight-fitting tube tops and halter tops. Bras had been gaining in popularity since the early part of the 1900s, as reformists continued to spread the word that corsets were the "root of all evil in womenswear."

Munsingwear's men's underpants line was limited to only a few offerings. One of Munsingwear's most popular men's items was the Skit-Suit: underpants "so brief, you don't know you're wearing them." The Skit-Suit featured a non-gap buttonless fly, elastic leg opening and waistband, and full seat coverage with an elastic drop seat. The Skit-Suit came in different lengths and fabrics, and it was upgraded at various times throughout the decades.

Sex and Silk Stockings

Advertising in the 1920s was becoming more and more daring for two simple reasons: sex sells, and so did silk stockings. Silk stockings like the ones Munsingwear made in this era inspired advertisers to push the boundaries of what was considered acceptable in print advertisements. Once silk stockings became available to the masses, and not just to the wealthy, hemlines shot up, perhaps specifically to show them off. Or maybe the new short skirts, which showed too much unsightly bare leg, made stockings a necessity, to cover up all that skin. Either way, advertisers responded by showing more leg in print ads, with the exception of one region. For whatever reason, the back of a woman's knee was considered sacrosanct, and no one in advertising dared cross this barometer of decency until 1925.

Once Munsingwear's competitor, Allen Hosiery, ran an ad showing the backs of not one but two knees, standards in advertising loosened up. To complement its new line of undergarments and hosiery, Munsingwear's ads in the 1920s and 1930s

McCall's Magazine, June 1929. Rayon was popular in 1920s fashion because it was cheaper and more durable than silk and felt cool and light against the skin, making it ideal for undergarments.

also took a sexy turn, with an occasional androgynous theme sprinkled in. This new, flirty Munsingwear contrasted starkly with the wholesome image the company projected.

In ads for Munsingwear's waterwear, men were depicted in one-piece suits with shoulder straps and a tight "skirt." Women wore very similar one-piece skirted suits. Aside from a few design elements, the biggest difference between the men's and women's swimsuits was that the women's suits had "sun-tops"—meaning the shoulder straps could be removed and the elastic-bodied suit would stay in place, so ladies could enjoy "a lovely unstreaked coat of tan." Other swimsuit manufacturers like Janzen and B.V.D. ran ads with strikingly similar imagery.

The Great Depression

As the nation fell deeper and deeper into an economic sinkhole in the late 1920s and 1930s, companies had to fight to collect even a few of the consumer's precious dollars. Munsingwear's secret weapon for surviving and even thriving during the Great Depression was Ruth M. Kapinas, underwear design guru.

Kapinas hailed from the New York School of Fine and Applied Art and established her own high-end line of handmade lingerie, which was available at retailers like Neiman Marcus and John Wanamaker. Upon joining Munsingwear, Kapinas experimented with the new "miracle yarn," Lastex—an elasticized yarn that could be knit or woven into rayon, nylon, silk, or cotton threads.

Kapinas designed Foundettes, an entirely new line of foundation garments that combined a brassiere and a girdle. Munsingwear installed special machines to produce this stretchy fabric that promised to be comfortable and light compared to the rigid steel stays, whalebone, and laces previously used in support undergarments.

Kapinas's patented Munsingwear Foundettes came in various styles and elastic strengths. These new undergarments were available in Lastex and rayon blends with cotton, silk, or worsted cotton. Foundettes were priced between $2.00 and $12.50 (a formidable amount in economically depressed times), depending on the style and amount of tension in the fabric.

After start-up losses in 1931 and 1932, when Foundettes were introduced, the garment became the major factor in Munsingwear's financial recovery. In fact, the company's profits grew despite the Great Depression. J. A. Munson, a

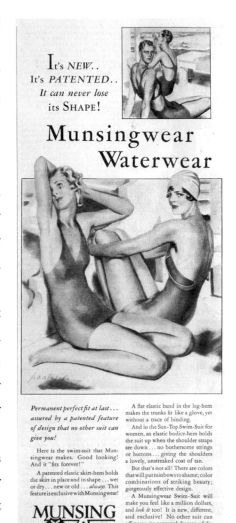

With "colors that will put the rainbows to shame," Munsingwear offered similar swimsuits for men and women in the 1920s.

PRICE
LIST

FALL AND WINTER
1934-1935

★

"Foundettes"

BY

MUNSING
Wear

★

Two-Way Stretch
Foundation Garments

New national advertising
and "Selling Helps"

★

THE MUNSINGWEAR
CORPORATION
Minneapolis, Minnesota
300 Fourth Ave., New York

ISSUED SEPTEMBER 10, 1934

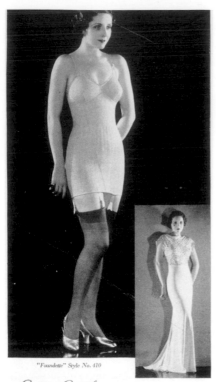

"Foundette" Style No. 410

Contour Control Not a ripple, not a bulge, if
Munsingwear "Foundettes" control your contour . . .
those lovely girdles and full-length foundation garments
that make you slimmer, trimmer, more comfortable.

"Foundettes" are knit as only Munsingwear can.
They're soft . . . smooth . . . and they stretch *two ways.*
They mould you . . . firmly, yet gently . . . into just the
contour you desire! Their
elastic strength defies
wear, they wash easily.
They're inexpensive, too
. . . girdles from $2.50 to
$7.50 for a full-length
foundation. At a quality
store near you. Mun-
singwear, Minneapolis.

Foundettes
BY
MUNSING
Wear

A Foundettes price list from
1934–35 carried the logo of the
National Recovery Authority,
showing the goods were
manufactured under the Corset
and Brassiere Code Authority.

Ad, early 1930s. Foundettes,
introduced during the Great
Depression, sold so well that
they helped Munsingwear keep
its bottom line intact.

Munsingwear merchandise manager, noted, "the sale of garments of this type
has increased very rapidly and they now occupy an important place in every
corset department."

In October 1937, Elizabeth Woodward, associate editor of *Ladies' Home
Journal,* had uncommonly high praise for Munsingwear's Foundettes: "Without
any preliminary fitting the garment is most comfortable. I like its lightweight,
attractive material, and the fine support which it gives. As a matter of actual fact
it has taken an inch off my waistline."

Another Foundettes fan and Munsingwear saleswoman, Alice Herzog, wrote to Kapinas personally to express appreciation: "It is the most comfortable garment I have ever had on and not any of the buyers believe I wear it until I show it to them. You know I am no featherweight and it does plenty for me."

Bras were also on the rise as the stock market fell, and Kapinas cleverly designed the Bando-Lure brassiere for the Foundette line. Instead of preshaped cups, which were the norm in 1930s bras, Kapinas engineered the stretchy rayon and Lastex fabric to create a tension that gave the "silhouette of lifted, separated breasts." The effect was a hammock-like uplift that created a sensation in the corset departments of upscale retailers.

Kapinas and her numerous Foundettes designs constituted a major coup for Munsingwear, yet the company and its workers faced other struggles during the Great Depression.

Unionization

Garment workers' unionization was a major concern for Munsingwear and its employees in the 1930s. The International Ladies' Garment Workers' Union (ILGWU), in particular, worked tirelessly from the turn of the century to the 1930s to get Munsingites to unionize, because Munsingwear employed thousands of garment workers who didn't have any formal representation in employee negotiations. Munsingwear was so leery of independent trade unions that it established its own union under the National Recovery Administration. Several Munsingwear officers served on a regional labor board and were given the power to block actions by employee unions, such as Munsingwear's.

Many Munsingites felt loyal to the company and desperately needed to keep their jobs during this time of economic turmoil, yet they also wanted better pay and benefits. Tension over unionization existed within the walls of the factory, in boardinghouses and pool halls, and in the streets of Minneapolis.

In 1935, a strike at the Minneapolis Strutwear Knitting Company, a maker of silk stockings, proved to be too close for Munsingites' comfort. The strike ignited after Strutwear cut employee wages and installed a company-run union.

Pickets and striking workers at the Strutwear Knitting Company, Minneapolis, 1935

Strutwear workers resisted and organized Local 38 of the American Federation of Full Fashioned Hosiery Workers. Almost immediately, eight workers were dismissed for their union organizing. Local 38 and union leaders called a strike, and the Strutwear plant was completely shut down.

On the fourth day of the strike, Strutwear tried to reopen, but three thousand workers and union supporters formed a massive picket line. Strikers staged a symbolic funeral for the death of Strutwear's company-run union, complete with a wooden coffin. Violence broke out when police escorts for the scab workers clubbed some of the strikers. Fearful that more violence would erupt on the picket line, Minnesota Governor Floyd B. Olson called out the National Guard.

The strike continued for eight months, leaving many workers with no income and few options. In early 1936, under pressure from city employers, the city welfare board denied hundreds of striking men and women their relief allowances as a means of getting them back to work. Social welfare organizations throughout Minneapolis and Hennepin County feared the worst for Strutwear's female employees. The Hennepin County Farmer-Labor Women's Club protested that the welfare board "had made an organized effort to force single girls who are on relief to accept jobs as domestics in homes at starvation wages, resulting in forcing these girls to accept employment at substandard wages and possibly forcing them into prostitution."

The daily struggles of the striking Strutwear employees made Munsingwear employees painfully aware of what they risked if they unionized. Conversely, Munsingwear officers, who agreed to sub-contract work for Strutwear, were acutely aware that they also risked a strike if they continued their anti-union position. In 1936 the ILGWU renewed organizing efforts with Munsingwear workers and within a year two hundred Munsingites signed on with the ILGWU. Still, this was not enough to mobilize all the employees. Instead, the company began negotiations with the Textile Workers Organization Committee, an initiative of the Committee for Industrial Organization (later the Congress of Industrial Organizations, or CIO), which led to a contract that offered minimal benefits to Munsingwear workers. Labor historians speculate that the Munsingwear employees who signed on with the ILGWU were pressured to break ties with that union or say good-bye to their jobs at Munsingwear.

According to Selma Kumpala, who started working for Munsingwear in 1925 and retired in 1970, "We joined because we had to." Kumpala recalled that most of the women were pleased about their arrangements for retirement and benefits. The young men, in her opinion, were eager for immediate wage increases. Kumpala also recalled that she and other female employees appreciated the respect Munsingwear showed them.

Despite the turmoil of the Depression, Munsingwear rounded out the 1930s on an upswing, introducing many technological advances to help modernize its machinery. The company overhauled its workflow processes in order to keep its competitive edge in the undergarment manufacturing industry. As the country debated its response to wars in Europe and Asia, Munsingwear was poised to do its part.

Munsingwear marching unit in the annual Aquatennial parade on Tenth Street South in Minneapolis on July 17, 1942

Skits, with a new design offering men a "stretchy seat," appeared in the 1941–42 Munsingwear price lists.

World War II

When the United States entered World War II in December of 1941, the spirit of patriotism in the country once again rose to epic levels. En masse, Americans enlisted in the armed services and civilians volunteered their time to plant victory gardens, organize blood drives, and salvage scrap metal for the war effort. Women were called to serve by taking jobs typically held by men, such as factory manufacturing.

Thirty-eight percent of Munsingwear's male employees enlisted for active duty, and several executives filled posts in Washington, advising the military on textiles. The Munsingwear factory held numerous Red Cross initiatives and bond drives. The company recruited women from around Minnesota to aid in the war effort through sewing and knitting because around-the-clock production was necessary to keep up with the wartime government contract. Half the production of Munsingwear went to military-issue underwear, and half of that was for wool underwear. Munsingwear also manufactured airplane wing covers, tents, hammocks, and mosquito netting for the war effort. In 1941, one of Munsingwear's subsidiaries, the David Clark Company in Worcester,

Massachusetts, developed an anti-G suit to protect pilots from blacking out during high-altitude flights by preventing blood from pooling in the lower body.

Munsingwear earned the Army and Navy "E" Flag for high achievement in war production on September 29, 1942. Clelland Simonson, president of Local 66 of the Textile Workers Organization Committee, accepted the award on behalf of the Munsingwear employees. Each Munsingite received a personal badge in honor of his or her commitment to the welfare of the United States.

Wartime manufacturing of some underwear, such as Munsingwear's Foundettes line, became problematic due to restrictions on rubber and elastic. Yet, wartime ads for Foundettes explained to women that it was their patriotic duty to look their best—and that meant wearing a girdle. One wartime ad titled "Smoke of Battle" features a slim, beautiful woman literally keeping the home fires burning—as she tends the fire in her high heels and Munsingwear Foundette. Its pitch is a fascinating piece of logic:

> In a soldier's emergency ration kit . . . with each grimly telescoped
> meal . . . four cigarettes are packed. Why? They will not keep a
> soldier alive. But our government knows that those cigarettes
> help to keep him fighting. To a woman, how well she looks is a
> barometer of how well she feels . . . how well she fights for Victory.
> With the restriction on rubber came this question: Are foundation
> garments essential? The government has answered that . . . by
> recognizing them as important to health and morale. Naturally,
> foundations today can't be made the same as before the war. Nor
> can there be so many of them. Isn't it sound then to buy those
> that are the finest . . . that will do the most for you? Munsingwear
> "Foundettes" are that kind.

The ad also includes a call to women to join war production. Munsingwear, like many advertisers, put a patriotic spin on other wartime ads, too, even if it took a gratuitous stretch. In one series of ads, women are pictured in military caps and underwear doing wartime work such as driving a truck and bandaging wounded

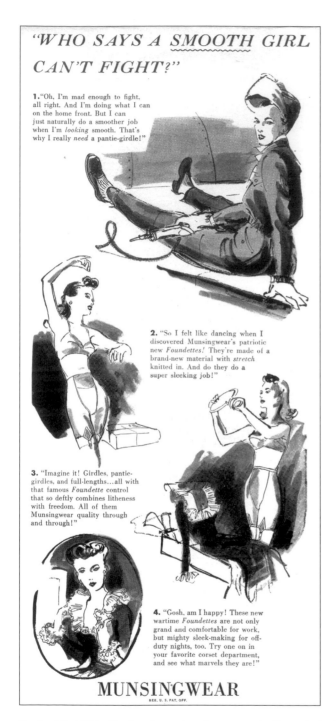

During World War II, advertisers played up romantically patriotic themes, even if the advertised item had no clear connection to the war effort. Munsingwear pointed out that its wartime prices were so low, "there's plenty change left for War Stamps and Bonds."

soldiers. The underwear promised to be "bulkless, petal-soft knitted cotton or rayon" because the "feminine touch is never more needed than now." And in a memorable wartime ad for Munsingwear Underlovlies, a nurse admires an x-ray that reveals the pink bra and panties of a woman who is getting a physical before she reports for her patriotic duty, proclaiming, "H'mmm . . . nothing wrong with her Munsingwear!"

Postwar Consumerism

The United States emerged from World War II as the most powerful nation in the world, and a nation that was ready to consume. In record numbers, Americans purchased cars, homes, televisions, mass-produced food items, and clothes. Advertising nurtured the desire for the new, continually persuaded Americans to consume more, at all costs, and led to the creation of a consumer culture, in which the consumption of unnecessary goods and services drives up the economy.

The garment industry greatly benefited from the postwar consumer culture it helped create. As Americans crowded department stores to purchase the abundant new clothing items, garment manufacturers like Munsingwear applied the processes and technology they had perfected for mass-producing military uniforms to keeping up with the postwar consumer demand for new, stylish clothes.

Ad, 1946. After the war, men could return to baseball and family life. "Whether you're tossing a few hot ones to Junior or waltzing with the wife at the Country Club, Munsingwear *follows through* with you."

Hollywood-Maxwell catalog, 1953. The whirlpool bra, claimed one ad, "gives you a TRUE full dimensional look whether nature gave you one or not."

In the 1950s, Munsingwear expanded its lingerie repertoire by acquiring the intimate apparel companies Vassar of Chicago and Hollywood-Maxwell of Los Angeles. Under the labels Hollywood Vassarette, Vassarette, and Munsingwear, the company ran the gamut of intimate apparel—from sensible and modest to fun, impractically beautiful, and everything in between. The company's whirlpool-stitch bras (also called bullet bras), nylon panties, lacy merry widows, chiffon peignoirs, and silk sleepwear were found in ads and editorials in all of the women's magazines.

Munsingwear's Vassarette line, known for keeping up with the fashion trends, quickly became a formidable force in the lingerie market, selling in all price points, in high-end department stores and mid-range clothing stores. The company even manufactured lingerie for the underwear underdog Frederick's of Hollywood. Frederick's was infamous for manufacturing underwear that was more about sex and less about practicality. Munsingwear, however, did not manufacture for Frederick's under any of the Munsingwear labels.

The company's lingerie routinely outsold the competition, due in large part to the leadership of Jean Norman Hall, the head Vassarette designer and the woman behind the underwear. Hall was one of the first designers to use gem-toned pattered fabrics and bold primary colors for lingerie and sleepwear. Hall kept Vassarette and Munsingwear on the cutting edge of fashion by traveling to Europe to preview fashion trends before they were introduced in America. She then incorporated the latest European styles in her fashion-forward designs.

Hall was also always looking back in garment history, to classic European styles, designs, fabrics, and embellishments. Inspired by antique French lace, Hall contracted with lace makers in Calais and Lyons to import large shipments of lace for use in Munsingwear's lingerie lines. She also visited lace museums in Switzerland and Italy, finding patterns in their collections that she wanted to reproduce for her lingerie designs back home. Upon returning to Minnesota, Hall helped to adapt Munsingwear's machinery to manufacture the complicated Swiss and Italian lace patterns for her delicate designs.

Pin-up ads, 1940s. After wartime restrictions on rubber were lifted, Munsingwear created an entirely new line of high-tension Foundettes that were manufactured with unforgiving, almost punishing, rubberized yarn. A woman no longer had to exercise to stay slim—her Foundette did the work.

Sex in Your Advertising and Chemistry in Your Underwear

To keep women thinking about those "younger lines," Munsingwear ran a series of ads that encouraged women to give up on trying to lose weight through exercise and buy Foundettes instead. The notion was a throwback to the Victorian era. However, the ads were anything but Victorian, picturing long-legged young women in suggestive "pinup" poses. In imagery that remains risqué even by today's standards, one woman in these ads "struggles" with exercise while a second woman—enveloped in a Foundette—lounges in her life of leisure.

The Vanishing American

AMERICAN WOMEN SPEND $675,000,000 on beauty every year. Part goes for face, hair, nails. The rest is spent on making figures finer with treatments and exercise. Improving figures *that* way is long and costly! Streamlining with Munsingwear foundation garments is the easier way to improve figures instantly!

FOR EVERY WOMAN FROM 14 TO 40, Munsingwear has a "Foundette" with the amazing 3-Way Control. Roundabout Stretch does the slimming. Vertical Stretch gives you comfort. Posture-Control helps to hold you in the lines of a natural, young figure! See what a Munsingwear "Foundette" can do for you today!

"Foundette" full-length #4388 of **Du Pont nylon,** *gored for comfortable control. Others, including pantie-girdles and girdles. Knit or woven of "Lastex" yarn. At better corset departments everywhere. Munsingwear, Inc., Minneapolis, New York, Chicago.*

MUNSINGWEAR
Foundettes
REG. U.S. PAT. OFF.

FOUNDATIONS FOR AGES 14 TO 40

Lazy Does It...Didn't It?

1. "What do you mean...*relax* and get a figure smooth as yours?"

2. "Let a Munsingwear *'Foundette'* do the work! First time I've ever had Figure-Appeal *and* this wonderful free feeling. That's 3-Way Control! It smooths down bulges, of course. But it also helps hold you in younger posture!"

3. *"Foundette" girdle #4070 (above), of power net with satin panels, is specially designed to give longer, lovelier lines. At better corset departments everywhere. Munsingwear, Inc., Minneapolis, New York, Chicago.*

MUNSINGWEAR
Foundettes
REG. U.S. PAT. OFF.

FOUNDATIONS FOR AGES 14 TO 40

The company's 1940s promotions for men also involved the art of storytelling. For today's readers, Munsingwear's "stretchy-seat" underwear campaign is almost shockingly homoerotic. For example, an ad shows two men wrestling in "stretchy-seat" underwear with the promise that it "gives up and down" and the headline, "Let's Get Down to Business."

Could readers of the 1940s, when gays were mostly closeted, possibly have noticed what readers of a later era see? Advertising historian Bruce H. Joffe argues that homosexuality may have been a taboo topic in our not-so-distant history, but allusions to homosexuality in advertising were pervasive and an effective advertising tool for companies intending to reach a broader market. Double entendres and buddy-bonding themes were often employed in the mainstream world of advertising. Ads for Cannon towels, Camel and Lucky Strike cigarettes, Van Heusen shirts, Schlitz beer, and underwear competitor B.V.D. also weren't shy about hinting at homosexuality.

"Let's Get Down to Business" ad, 1945: "Men find it so comfortable they keep coming back for more."

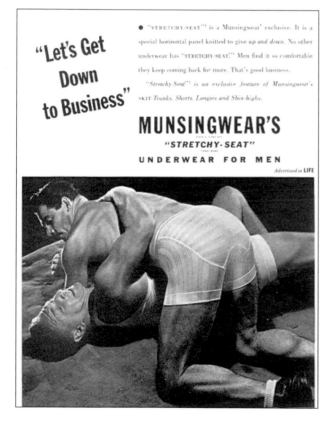

These themes became especially complicated when advertising men's underwear. Underwear is inextricably associated with morality, modesty, lack of modesty, sexuality, hygiene, and social status—and it is forever at the whim of fashion.

Munsingwear didn't appear to take itself too seriously, though, using humor while pushing the boundaries. Joffe notes, "Wink-wink went Munsingwear's ads throughout the 1940s, deliberately cranking up the bawdy and risqué with humorous headlines, dialogue, and photos of men in close quarters cracking jokes about their naked cover-ups. Half-dressed, bare-chested men taking liberties in these ads made asses out of themselves—literally and figuratively—in and out of their underwear."

"Best Seat in the House...Sez You!"

SANDY: Yes, sez I! And why? Because this seat is Munsingwear's new "Stretchy-Seat,"* a special panel knitted to stretch up and down...a patented, exclusive feature. Bend over and it gives plenty. Straighten up, and it comes right back.

JIM: Another scoop for Munsingwear, I admit. But I get freedom and ease aplenty in these Munsingwear "BREEX."* They're bias-cut, free-flowing champions, and don't forget it.

SANDY: Well, here's another Munsingwear bull's-eye...the SKIT-Winger Shirt. Crew neck, short sleeves, wear it solo for sports if you like. A great little torso-trap, believe me!

JIM: Nix for me! I'm strong for the sleeveless type...Munsingwear's Athletic Shirt. Fits like my skin and gives with every move. A Munsingwear masterpiece, no foolin'.

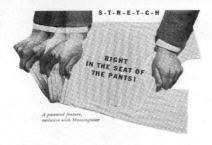

S—T—R—E—T—C—H

RIGHT IN THE SEAT OF THE PANTS!

A patented feature, exclusive with Munsingwear

MUNSINGWEAR'S

NEW "STRETCHY-SEAT"* UNDERWEAR FOR MEN

"Old Flappy-Pants-Pappy Himself!"

PETE: Can the comedy, will you? These suit me, and I like 'em...get it? They're Munsingwear "BREEX."* They're bias-cut, with as much room and comfort behind as anybody needs...and what about that stingy little number *you* got on?

MAC: Stingy, my eye! You mean streamlined, modern...what a getting-around guy needs. Munsingwear, too...these SKIT-Shorts, with the new, easy "Stretchy-Seat"* that stretches up and down.

PETE: Say, I'll still back my "BREEX"* against the world. But you must have *some* sense; I see you wear Munsingwear's Athletic Shirt.

MAC: No, this is Munsingwear's SKIT-Shirt, shaped to fit the shorts. It's an active man's best friend...fits like my skin and gives with every move.

S—T—R—E—T—C—H

RIGHT IN THE SEAT OF THE PANTS!

A patented feature, exclusive with Munsingwear

MUNSINGWEAR'S

NEW "STRETCHY-SEAT"* UNDERWEAR FOR MEN.

In ads of the 1940s, "active" men teased one another about their choice of Munsingwear men's undergarments. Munsingwear's "athletic shirts" were designed to be tucked into either Breex or Skit-shorts.

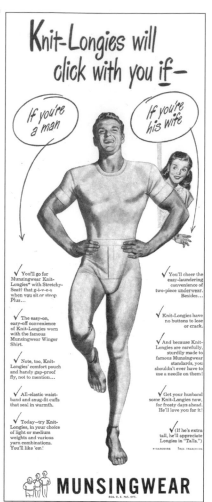

Green T-shirt ad, 1955. Munsingwear's patented nylon-reinforced neckbands revolutionized men's undershirts. Nylon neckbands did not sag, and they lasted much longer than the competitors' t-shirts.

Comfort two ways ad, 1951

Knit-Longies ad, 1950s

Munsingwear also ran a series of ads with men teasing one another in bedrooms, locker rooms, and dugouts about their choice of underwear. Another series of ads showed men defending their Munsingwear underwear styles. In one, the headline reads, "Best Seat in the House . . . Sez You!" An underwear-clad man is on his hands and knees with his backside to the camera while his similarly dressed friend stands over him. Joffe points out that the playful repartee takes place in front of an unmade, full-sized bed that the two gentlemen presumably share.

Underwear designs were evolving thanks to a good dose of chemistry. For women, Munsingwear introduced Stay There foundation fashions, made with more rigid elastic and Ban-Lon, a synthetic yarn, to provide more body "cling" and elasticity. Stay There was ideal in bras, especially strapless bras, offering women the "security" of non-slip support. The popular sweater girl of the 1950s, with her gravity-defying lift and silhouette, was born.

A little chemistry also found its way into Munsingwear's line of men's underwear. Nylon gave the neckbands of undershirts greater elasticity, yet they retained their shape. And DuPont nylon and Lastex were added for stretch and comfort in men's Skit-trunks, shorts, Longies, and Shin-high underpants.

Coordination Nation

Selling Mrs. Consumer on the concept of coordinating her underwear with her outerwear was of the utmost importance in the postwar era. The premise was simple: it wasn't just fashionable, it was *proper* for women to coordinate their

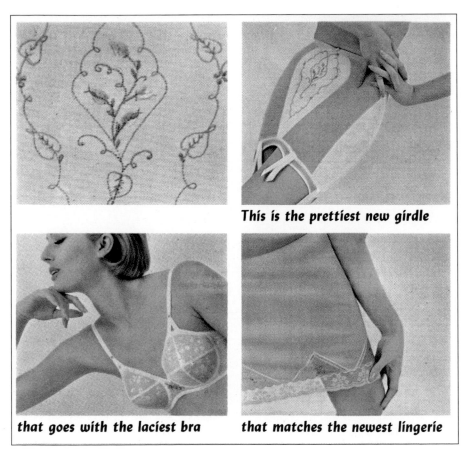

Detail of Hollywood Vassarette Coordinates ad, 1965

This is the prettiest new girdle

that goes with the laciest bra

that matches the newest lingerie

"Let's take the confusion out of coordination," promised the Hollywood Vassarette Lingerie and Sleepwear catalog for fall and winter 1963. It touted "such innovations as colors which relate inner-fashion to outerwear" and showed retailers a lovely lineup of garments.

HOLLYWOOD
Vassarette

NYLON TRICOT PEIGNOIR AND GOWN SETS

Designer Line

STYLE 6305
'Antonia'
Peignoir & Gown Set

- Madeira hand-embroidered and hand-padded rosebuds on peignoir bodice
- Imported Valenciennes nylon lace
- Double-layered nylon chiffon throughout
- Subtle smocking at bodice
- Yoke extends to form a slightly capped sleeve
- French binding at neckline, sleeves and hem
- Sold only as a set with Waltz Gown 6295 shown on page 41

COLORS:
Sachet Pink/White Yoke/ White Lace
White/White Yoke/White Lace

STYLE 6303
'Melissa' Peignoir & Gown Set

- Imported hand-cut French lace
- Intricate lace appliques at shallow neckline, shoulder, pocket
- Double puff sleeve
- French binding
- Pearl buttons
- Matching lace appliqued waltz gown
- Sold only as a set with Waltz Gown 6263 on page 40

COLORS:
Aqua Frost
Black
Breezy Blue
Sachet Pink
White

Style No.	Service Class	Boxed	Sizes	Price	Sugg. Retail	Retail Mark-up %
6303	X	1/12 Gown 1/12 Peignoir	32-38	$212.00	$35.00	50.0

Style No.	Service Class	Boxed	Sizes	Price	Sugg. Retail	Retail Mark-up %
6305	X	1/12 Waltz Gown 1/12 Peignoir	S-M-L	$260.00	$39.95	46.3

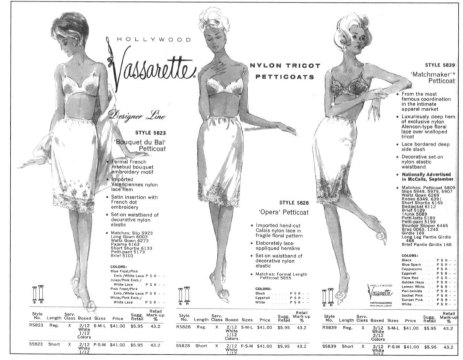

HOLLYWOOD
Vassarette

NYLON TRICOT PETTICOATS

Designer Line

STYLE 5823
'Bouquet du Bal' Petticoat

- Formal French rosebud bouquet embroidery motif
- Imported Valenciennes nylon lace hem
- Satin insertion with French dot embroidery
- Set-on waistband of decorative nylon elastic
- Matches: Slip 5923 Long Gown 6003 Waltz Gown 6273 Pajama 6163 Short Shortie 6133 Petti-pant 5173 Brief 5103

COLORS:
Blue Frost/Pink Emb./White Lace P S R - -
Julep/Pink Emb./ White Lace P S R - -
Pink Frost/Pink Emb./White Lace P S R - -
White/Pink Emb./ White Lace P S R - -

STYLE 5828
'Opera' Petticoat

- Imported hand-cut Calais nylon lace in fragile floral pattern
- Elaborately lace-appliqued hemline
- Set-on waistband of decorative nylon elastic
- Matches: Formal Length Petticoat 5855

COLORS:
Black P S R - -
Eggshell P S R - -
White P S R - -

STYLE 5839
'Matchmaker'* Petticoat

- From the most famous coordination in the intimate apparel market
- Luxuriously deep hem of exclusive nylon Alencon-type floral lace over scalloped tricot
- Lace bordered deep side slash
- Decorative set-on nylon elastic waistband
- **Nationally Advertised in McCall's, September**
- Matches: Petticoat 5809 Slips 5949, 5979, 5907 Waltz Gown 6269 Robes 6349, 6391 Short Shortie 6169 Bedjacket 6112 Brief 5109 Trunk 5089 Petti-lotte 5189 Petti-pant 5199 Boudoir Slipper 6465 Bras 0063, 1245 Girdle 169 Long Leg Pantie Girdle 468 Brief Pantie Girdle 168

COLORS:
Black P S R - -
Blue Spark P S R - -
Cappuccino P S R - -
Eggshell P S R - -
Flare Red P S R - -
Golden Haze P S R - -
Lemon White P S R - -
Peri-twinkle P S R - -
Sachet Pink P S R - -
Sunset Pink P S R - -
White P S R - -

HOLLYWOOD
Vassarette
MATCHMAKERS

Style No.	Length	Serv. Class	Boxed	Sizes	Price	Sugg. Retail	Retail Mark-up %
R5823	Reg.	X	2/12 White 1/12 Colors	S-M-L	$41.00	$5.95	43.2
S5823	Short	X	2/12 White 1/12	P-S-M	$41.00	$5.95	43.2

Style No.	Length	Serv. Class	Boxed	Sizes	Price	Sugg. Retail	Retail Mark-up %
R5828	Reg.	X	2/12 White 1/12	S-M-L	$41.00	$5.95	43.2
S5828	Short	X	2/12 White 1/12	P-S-M	$41.00	$5.95	43.2

Style No.	Length	Serv. Class	Boxed	Sizes	Price	Sugg. Retail	Retail Mark-up %
R5839	Reg.	X	3/12 White 2/12 Colors	S-M-L	$41.00	$5.95	43.2
S5839	Short	X	3/12 White 2/12	P-S-M	$41.00	$5.95	43.2

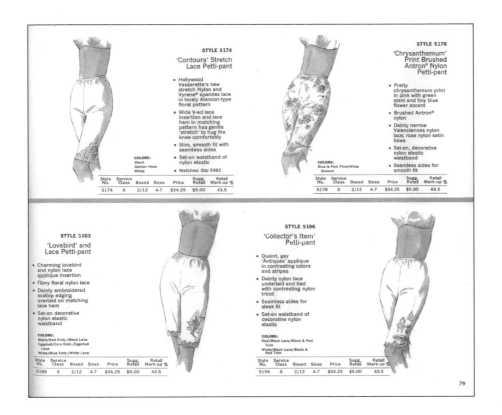

STYLE 5174

'Contoura' Stretch
Lace Petti-pant

- Hollywood
  Vassarette's new
  stretch Nylon and
  Vyrene® spandex lace
  in lovely Alencon-type
  floral pattern
- Wide V-ed lace
  insertion and lace
  hem in matching
  pattern has gentle
  'stretch' to hug the
  knee comfortably
- Slim, smooth fit with
  seamless sides
- Set-on waistband of
  nylon elastic
- Matches: Slip 5982

COLORS:
Black
Golden Haze
White

Style No.	Service Class	Boxed	Sizes	Price	Sugg. Retail	Retail Mark-up %
5174	X	2/12	4-7	$34.25	$5.00	43.5

STYLE 5178

'Chrysanthemum'
Print Brushed
Antron® Nylon
Petti-pant

- Pretty
  chrysanthemum print
  in pink with green
  stem and tiny blue
  flower accent
- Brushed Antron®
  nylon
- Dainty narrow
  Valenciennes nylon
  lace; rose nylon satin
  bows
- Set-on, decorative
  nylon elastic
  waistband
- Seamless sides for
  smooth fit

COLORS:
Blue & Pink Print/White
Ground

Style No.	Service Class	Boxed	Sizes	Price	Sugg. Retail	Retail Mark-up %
5178	X	2/12	4-7	$34.25	$5.00	43.5

STYLE 5183

'Lovebird' and
Lace Petti-pant

- Charming lovebird
  and nylon lace
  applique insertion
- Filmy floral nylon lace
- Dainty embroidered
  scallop edging
  overlaid on matching
  lace hem
- Set-on decorative
  nylon elastic
  waistband

COLORS:
Black/Red Emb./Black Lace
Eggshell/Ecru Emb./Eggshell
  Lace
White/Blue Emb./White Lace

Style No.	Service Class	Boxed	Sizes	Price	Sugg. Retail	Retail Mark-up %
5183	X	2/12	4-7	$34.25	$5.00	43.5

STYLE 5196

'Collector's Item'
Petti-pant

- Quaint, gay
  'Antiques' applique
  in contrasting colors
  and stripes
- Dainty nylon lace
  underlaid and tied
  with contrasting nylon
  tricot
- Seamless sides for
  sleek fit
- Set-on waistband of
  decorative nylon
  elastic

COLORS:
Red/Black Lace/Black & Red
  Trim
White/Black Lace/Black &
  Red Trim

Style No.	Service Class	Boxed	Sizes	Price	Sugg. Retail	Retail Mark-up %
5196	X	2/12	4-7	$34.25	$5.00	43.5

79

purses, shoes, and gloves—in color, style, and material. Garment manufacturers advertised the fairy tale that a well-bred woman was a well-coordinated woman who could harmonize her entire household, including her under-things. She would never consider wearing a beige slip under a black dress. And the coordinating didn't stop there; panties and bras were sold in sets with matching garter belts, girdles, and slips.

The concept required a truly challenging level of coordination within the company. Designers in the studios for girdles, bras, and lingerie cooperated on matching details of color, lace, and trim; researchers found ways to match the colors of fabrics, threads, and laces; and the sales force learned the details of *which-matched-what* to spread the word.

Munsingwear's entire line of coordinated ensembles of lingerie, foundation wear, and brassieres, known as Matchmakers, proved to be very popular with shoppers, as was a romantic line of robes and matching nightgowns known as

The idea for Munsingwear's Slenderella stockings was born in the late 1950s, when a company rep saw a Hollywood body makeup artist applying makeup to an actress's legs. Soon after, subtle shading was added to Munsingwear's nylon stockings, creating the illusion of shapelier legs.

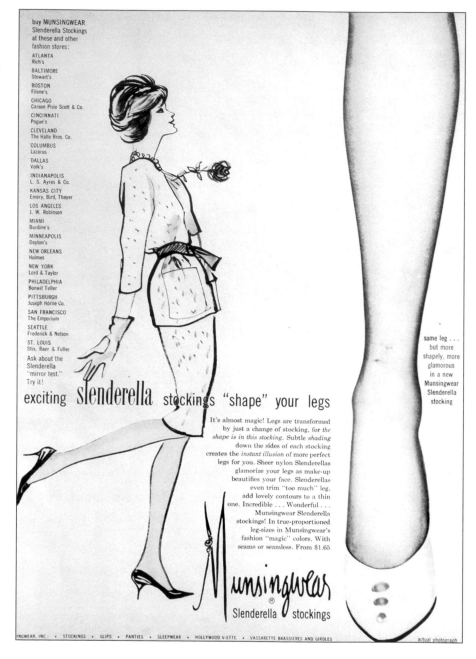

buy MUNSINGWEAR Slenderella Stockings at these and other fashion stores:

ATLANTA
Rich's
BALTIMORE
Stewart's
BOSTON
Filene's
CHICAGO
Carson Pirie Scott & Co.
CINCINNATI
Pogue's
CLEVELAND
The Halle Bros. Co.
COLUMBUS
Lazarus
DALLAS
Volk's
INDIANAPOLIS
L. S. Ayres & Co.
KANSAS CITY
Emery, Bird, Thayer
LOS ANGELES
J. W. Robinson
MIAMI
Burdine's
MINNEAPOLIS
Dayton's
NEW ORLEANS
Holmes
NEW YORK
Lord & Taylor
PHILADELPHIA
Bonwit Teller
PITTSBURGH
Joseph Horne Co.
SAN FRANCISCO
The Emporium
SEATTLE
Frederick & Nelson
ST. LOUIS
Stix, Baer & Fuller
Ask about the Slenderella "mirror test." Try it!

same leg . . . but more shapely, more glamorous in a new Munsingwear Slenderella stocking

exciting Slenderella stockings "shape" your legs

It's almost magic! Legs are transformed by just a change of stocking, for *the shape is in this stocking*. Subtle *shading* down the sides of each stocking creates the *instant illusion* of more perfect legs for you. Sheer nylon Slenderellas glamorize your legs as make-up beautifies your face. Slenderellas even trim "too much" leg, add lovely contours to a thin one. Incredible . . . Wonderful . . . Munsingwear Slenderella stockings! In true-proportioned leg-sizes in Munsingwear's fashion "magic" colors. With seams or seamless. From $1.65

Munsingwear
®
Slenderella stockings

INGWEAR, INC. · STOCKINGS · SLIPS · PANTIES · SLEEPWEAR · HOLLYWOOD V-ETTE · VASSARETTE BRASSIERES AND GIRDLES   actual photograph

Candleglow. Munsingwear also sold matching mother-and-daughter sleepwear and father-and-son pajamas, slippers, and robe sets.

Garment coordination—in particular, matching underwear ensembles—was a key marketing strategy in the garment industry. By making women feel special and put-together—inside and out—garment companies like Munsingwear could boost sales of unessential undergarments that seemed somehow impossible to live without. Women were, indeed, in the mood for Munsingwear.

The Penguin

As famous as Munsingwear was for manufacturing underwear, it was a little penguin logo that turned Munsingwear into a twentieth-century fashion icon. In 1955, Munsingwear introduced a new line, the Grand Slam knit golf shirt, with a little penguin embroidered on it. The origins of Pete the Penguin have reached legendary, if not exaggerated proportions. As the story goes, Munsingwear salesman extraordinaire Abbot Pederson was drunk on a business trip to New York when he made an impulse purchase from a Manhattan taxidermist: a stuffed penguin. Pederson named the penguin "Pete" and took it to a meeting with a new idea for a golf shirt to go up against the popular French Lacoste brand, with its iconic crocodile.

Pete the Penguin

The Grand Slam golf shirt with the penguin logo was famously worn by golf enthusiasts Bob Hope, Dean Martin, and Bing Crosby as well as by golfing legend Arnold Palmer. This casual, permanent-press shirt became a classic both on and off the golf course. While not as fashionable as the Lacoste brand, the Grand Slam was favored among avid golfers because the golf-minded Munsingwear designers, after surveying 240 golf professionals, added an "action gusset"—a ribbed slice of fabric on the underarm to avoid any interference with the golf swing—and throughout the 1960s and 1970s Grand Slam sport shirts were estimated to be the best-selling golf shirt in the world.

Capitalizing on this success, Munsingwear added bowling shirts to its offerings around 1958. Similar to golf shirts, but with a bowling penguin logo, they were worn by Richard Nixon and Frank Sinatra and loved for their casual sport fashion statement and their kitsch quotient. Still not having exhausted the potential of the little bird, Munsingwear introduced a lady penguin logo to a new line of women's golf, bowling, and fashion shirts.

Throughout the 1960s and 1970s, Munsingwear cranked out new designs,

Ad, 1972. The Knitpeople
enjoy the winning comfort of
Grand Slam sportswear.

THE KNITPEOPLE: TOP MONEY WINNERS YEAR AFTER YEAR.
It's true. Every year the Knitpeople make every other golf knit look second best. It's
happened again. Munsingwear's Grand-Slam® Sportswear Collection '72 is filled with
great new polyester doubleknit shirts, slacks and sweaters. All winners. All coordinated
beautifully. Collars and plackets match the slacks. Let's face it. In golfing or knitting, winner takes all. And the winner is always the Knitpeople.

munsingwear

Grand-Slam Sportswear Collection/Minneapolis, Minn. 55405 • New York: 135 West 50th St.

new offerings, and new innovations—like hidden zippers. Sales continued
to be healthy in these decades, but earnings were slipping, and many feared
the worst for the Munsingwear Corporation. In addition to the Minneapolis
plant, Munsingwear manufactured garments in fifteen locations in Minnesota,

Wisconsin, Alabama, Arkansas, Oklahoma, Texas, and Illinois—all in jeopardy of closing their doors.

North Minneapolis Bids Farewell

When Munsingwear's earnings lost traction through the 1970s, industry insiders chalked it up to "revolving door management" and the lack of solid marketing strategies. Others blamed lifestyle changes, as a new generation of women abandoned their mother's and grandmother's foundation garments, significantly weakening the Vassarette division.

Munsingwear found it increasingly difficult to remain relevant with consumers as the garment industry became more fragmented and advertising became savvier. New designer jeans and logoed shirts flooded the market, creating fresh, "must-have" brands. To a new generation of consumers, the penguin logo seemed hopelessly outdated.

While other garment manufacturers moved to cheaper offshore sites, Munsingwear continued the vast majority of its production in the United States, operating fabric plants and manufacturing facilities. Despite appeals from Minneapolis mayor Don Fraser and the local textile union, and a swelling public outcry from the North Minneapolis community, the Munsingwear factory in Minneapolis shut its doors in 1981, and company headquarters moved across town. Munsingwear would continue in various incarnations, but this fact was small comfort to the four hundred employees who lost their jobs.

The Munsingwear factory's workings were dismantled, machinery was shipped out, and corporate files along with an impressive collection of salesman's samples and other artifacts were donated to the Minnesota Historical Society. It took almost a year for workers to unthread the knitting machines, remove mammoth rolls and bolts of fabric, and pack up stockpiles of yarns, buttons, and bows. Author Kathryn Strand Koutsky writes of the final day: "When the moving crew closed the gates for the last time, the 70-year-old factory buildings were empty for the first time. A hollow silence replaced the noisy whir of knitting machinery and the animated chatter of textile workers. No one was left to

Designers now fill International Market Square, former home of Munsingwear and the Northwestern Knitting Company. The building's entrance was built through the former powerhouse.

wrinkle a nose at fumes from the bleach vats, or wince when boxcar wheels screeched along the rails. Minnesota's famous knitting mill was gone."

Shortly after the factory closed, the Munsingwear complex was listed on the National Register of Historic Places and plans were under way for a massive adaptive reuse renovation project.

In 1985 a new complex rose in Munsingwear's place: International Market Square, housing offices, showrooms, shops, a restaurant, and an impressive five-story atrium where the old courtyard and railroad tracks used to be. In 2005, a portion of the building was renovated again to make ninety-six loft apartments. It is still Minnesota's largest renovated building, housing over seventy design-related showrooms.

For almost one hundred years Munsingwear made its indelible mark on Minnesota and Minnesota did the same for Munsingwear. The two histories are intertwined, and together they shaped the way America thought about, purchased, and wore underwear. As underwear evolved over the past century, Munsingwear not only kept pace but also outpaced the industry with offerings that were ahead of their time.

The Munsingwear name lives on with the resurgence of vintage fashion; retro seekers comb thrift stores for the coveted Munsingwear and Vassarette labels—a testament to enduring design and quality. And Munsingwear's infamous Pete the Penguin made a whip-smart comeback in 2003, gracing a new collection of vintage-inspired sportswear, aptly named Original Penguin by Munsingwear.

The atrium at International Market Square, where railcars were once filled with goods

ACKNOWLEDGMENTS

Researching "underneath it all" was like a party, complete with an impressive guest list of individuals who enthusiastically provided support, help, encouragement, humor, and superior attention to detail.

I am deeply indebted to the following:

Ann Regan, Minnesota Historical Society Press

Linda McShannock, Minnesota Historical Society

Dave Stevens, Mill City Museum, Minnesota Historical Society

Kate Roberts, Minnesota Historical Society

Shannon Pennefeather, Minnesota Historical Society Press

Aleah Vinick, Minnesota Historical Society

Helen Newlin, Minnesota Historical Society Press

Heather Block Lawson, James K. Hosmer Special Collections,
    Hennepin County Library

Eileen Roberts, William Mitchell College of Law

Janelle Beitz, William Mitchell College of Law

Minnesota Historical Society library staff

Barbara Mikkelson, Snopes.com

Susan Larson, Minnesota State Law Library

Sara Wakefield, Immigration History Research Center,
    University of Minnesota

Barbara Shelton

John Kurtis Dehn

Chuck Olsen

Wenonah Wilms

Ed Wilms

Alice Marks

Sam Marks

Jane Marks-Hastig

Robert Marks-Kerst

And a good time (I hope!) was had by all.

SOURCE NOTES

The Minnesota Historical Society holds the Munsingwear, Inc., Corporate Records, 1887–1995 (hereafter Munsingwear Records). Company materials cited below may be found either in this manuscript collection or in the society's reference library.

1. UNMENTIONABLE

For general background on Munsingwear, Inc., see Charles Pillsbury, "Munsingwear: Its Ideals and Development," April 1923, in Historical Information, Munsingwear Records; William C. Edgar, "The Song of Munsingwear," in *Minneapolis Golden Jubilee, 1867–1917, A History of Fifty Years of Civic and Commercial Progress* (Minneapolis: Tribune Printing, 1917), 56–59; *The Story of Munsingwear since 1886* (Minneapolis: The Company, 1964); Evadene Burris Swanson, "Don't Say 'Underwear,' Say 'Munsingwear,'" *Hennepin County History* (Winter 1987): 10; Marcia G. Anderson, "Munsingwear: An Underwear for America," *Minnesota History* 50 (Winter 1986): 152–61. Early letters of discontent are in Northwestern Knitting Company correspondence files, [ca. 188-]–1895, Munsingwear Records.

    Eva Gay. Valesh's story is in the *St. Paul Globe*, May 6, 1888, p. 1–2. For more on her undercover journalism, see Elizabeth Faue, *Writing the Wrongs: Eva Valesh and the Rise of Labor Journalism* (Ithaca, NY: Cornell University Press, 2002), 17–30. On the Chicago Garment Workers Strike, see http://timelines.com/1910/9/22/chicago-garment-workers-strike; on the Triangle Shirtwaist Fire, see David von Drehle, *Triangle: The Fire That Changed America* (New York: Grove Press,

2004), and http://www.ilr.cornell.edu/trianglefire/narrative3.html. The fire was considered the worst workplace disaster in New York until the terrorist attacks on the World Trade Center on September 11, 2001 (http://www.labor.ny.gov/agencyinfo/PDFs/9-11_WPTF_Annual_Report_2009_0601.pdf).

2. What's Under There?

A helpful history of underwear and the Dress Reform Movement is Jane Farrell-Beck and Colleen Gau's *Uplift: The Bra in America* (Philadelphia: University of Pennsylvania Press, 2002) and Patricia A. Cunningham, *Reforming Women's Fashion, 1850–1920: Politics, Health and Art* (Kent, OH: Kent State University Press, 2003), 79, 89. Early forms of the brassiere were patented in America in 1876 (Farrell-Beck and Gau, p. 5).

Advertising Under There. Sample ads from competitors are in Advertising and Sales Promotion materials, Munsingwear Records.

"The Largest Knitting Mill." On the growth of the company and its new facilities, see Edgar, "Song of Munsingwear," 56–59, and Clarence Tolg, "The Lore of Uncle Fogy: Reminiscences, Philosophy and Some Practical Advice from a Fine Old Gentleman, Clarence Tolg" (Minneapolis: Munsingwear, Inc., and WCCO Radio, 1971). Tolg, a former Munsingwear vice president, wrote affectionately about the steam whistle.

The Case of the Missing Underwear. The underwear detective's reports are in Investigative Reports, William J. Burns Detective Agency, October-December 1915, Munsingwear Records; the final bill shows a deduction of $37.82 paid to Operative #71 as wages during the five weeks. On the Citizens Alliance, see the foreword by Mary Lethert Wingerd to Charles Rumford Walker, *American City: A Rank and File History of Minneapolis* (Minneapolis: University of Minnesota Press, 2005), 4; also William Millikan, *A Union Against Unions: The Minneapolis Citizens Alliance and Its Fight Against Organized Labor, 1903–1947* (St. Paul: Minnesota Historical Society Press, 2003).

3. MUNSINGITE

On the company's World War I history, see Anderson, "Munsingwear," 160; *Munsingwear News* (hereafter *MW News*), January 1919, p. 9 ("'This has been a wonderful time,'" and "manufacturing over 82,000 compresses"). The size of the company's labor force is discussed in Anderson, "Munsingwear," 152.

For Munsingites as "100% Americans," "becoming better Americans," the list of company classes offered, and "other subjects," see *The Success of Well Doing,* a booklet "issued in lieu of one of the regular 1921 issues" of *MW News,* 51. Hulda Koskie's essay is in *MW News,* April 1920, p. 12. For "Only once did I sew" and information on preferential treatment of the American born, see Lars Olsson, "Evelina Johansdotter, Textile Workers, and the Munsingwear Family: Class, Gender, and Ethnicity in the Political Economy of Minnesota at the End of World War I," in Philip J. Anderson and Dag Blanck, eds., *Swedes in the Twin Cities: Immigrant Life and Minnesota's Urban Frontier* (St. Paul: Minnesota Historical Society Press, 2001), 83–86.

For publicity materials touting "happy surroundings," "wholesome enthusiasm," and "every courtesy," see *Success of Well Doing,* 7. Edgar, "Song of Munsingwear," 57, describes the typical female Munsingite. Johansdotter's account is translated and quoted in Olsson, "Evelina Johansdotter, Textile Workers, and the Munsingwear Family," 77–90 (quotations p. 84).

On the medical department and "friendly visitor," see *Success of Well Doing,* 43, 47. Elizabeth Faue, *Community of Suffering & Struggle: Women, Men and the Labor Movement in Minneapolis, 1915–1945* (Raleigh: University of North Carolina Press, 1991), 23, discusses the migration of young women to the Twin Cities. On the social service department and various employee social and sports activities, see *Success of Well Doing,* 37, 39.

Munsingwear News. For quotations about the newsletter, see *Success of Well Doing,* 49, and the various issues cited in the text. *Munsingwear News* was renamed *Munsingwear Briefs* in 1966. On gardening, see *MW News,* April 1920, p. 10. The library issue was published April 1920 ("It's up to you," p. 26); see also *Success of Well Doing,* 41 ("There are times"). Burris, "Don't Say 'Underwear,'" 7, discusses Sowell and Chatfield; see also Marilyn Revell DeLong, ed., *Minnesota Creates: Fashion for a Century* (St. Paul: Goldstein Museum of Design, University of Minnesota, 2000), 54–56.

4. IN THE MOOD FOR MUNSINGWEAR

Design: On Spilsbury, see Pillsbury, "Munsingwear: Its Ideals and Development." The work of the design department is described in "How Munsingwear Makes Underwear" (copy of a typed brochure for Munsingwear's sales force, c. 1940), 8 ("Now it is essential"), and *The Curtain Rises on Munsingwear Modes* (Minneapolis: The Company, [1920]), [15] ("cleverly designed"). On bras and corsets, see Farrell-Beck and Gau, *Uplift,* 4 ("root of all evil"), 5.

Sex and Silk Stockings. Charles Goodrum and Helen Dalrymple, *Advertising in America: The First Two Hundred Years* (New York: Harry N. Abrams, Inc., 1990), 71, 73, discuss the advertising of silk stockings.

The Great Depression. Kapinas is discussed in Heidi L. Boehlke, "Ruth M. Kapinas, Munsingwear's Forgotten 'Foundettes' Designer," *Dress Magazine* 20 (1993): 48 ("the sale of garments," "Without any preliminary," and "It is the most comfortable"), and Farrell-Beck and Gau, *Uplift,* 78–79 ("silhouette").

Unionization. On unionization and the Strutwear strike, see Faue, *Community of Suffering & Struggle,* 117, 120 ("organized effort to force"), 121, 130–31, and Burris, "Don't Say 'Underwear,'" 14 ("we joined because").

World War II. On Munsingwear in World War II, see Burris, "Don't Say 'Underwear,'" 14, and Kathryn Strand Koutsky, *Munsingwear and International Market Square: Celebrating the Buildings' First One Hundred Years, 1904–2004* (London: Portobello Press, 2004), 59.

Postwar Consumerism. For Hall's obituary, see Steve Kopperud, "She cut the undies short but not before the dye vat," *Minneapolis Star,* June 7, 1973.

Sex in Your Advertising. For discussions of homoeroticism in Munsingwear's ads, see Bruce H. Joffe, *A Hint of Homosexuality? 'Gay' and Homoerotic Imagery in American Print Advertising* (Bloomington, IN: Xlibris Company, 2007), 7, 8, 29, 61–79, 161–62, 179 ("Wink wink").

Coordination Nation. On matching ensembles, see DeLong, ed., *Minnesota Creates*, 54–56; *Story of Munsingwear*, 53–54.

The Penguin. See *Story of Munsingwear*, 52; Koutsky, *Munsingwear and International Market Square*, 56. On the later decades, see Swanson, "Don't Say 'Underwear,'" 10; Anderson, "Munsingwear," 61; *Story of Munsingwear*, 53–60.

North Minneapolis Bids Farewell. On Munsingwear's decline in Minnesota, see Burris, "Don't Say 'Underwear,'" 3–4, 18; Jeffrey A. Trachtenberg, "The Minnow and the Basses," *Forbes*, February 25, 1985, p. 75; Eleanor Johnson Tracy, "Stodgy Munsingwear Changes Its Underwear," *Fortune*, September 3, 1984, p. 67; and Dick Youngblood, "Smaller Is Better," (Minneapolis) *StarTribune*, January 26, 1998, p. 1D. Koutsky, *Munsingwear and International Market Square*, p. 20–21 ("When the moving crew").

INDEX

Page numbers in *italic* refer to illustrations

ILLUSTRATION CREDITS

The photographs on p. 102–4 were provided courtesy International Market Square. All other materials are from the collections of the Minnesota Historical Society.

Museum Collections
p. ii: women's union suits, left, 1984.112.495, right, 1984.112.119; p. 29: box, 1984.112.185; p. 53: man's union suit, 1984.112.575; p. 55: paper dolls, 1997.114.1; p. 59: Foundettes, 1984.112.11; p. 60: flag bra and girdle, 1990.203.1; p. 62: bra, 1984.112.2001, panties, 1992.30.19; p. 63: merry widow, 1984.112.2392, girdle, 1984.112.1659; p. 64: slip, 1990.497.24; p. 65: peignoir and gown, 1990.203.78; p. 67: Toulouse coordinates, 1992.30.5 a-c.

Munsingwear, Inc., Corporate Records
Ads on p. vi, xi, 3, 5, 17, 18, 20, 22, 31, 54, 56, 57, 58, 61, 66, 68, 71, 72, 76, 77, 78, 79, 80, 84 (Skits), 86, 87, 90, 91, 93, 94, 98, 99, 100, 106: Advertising and sales promotion, Magazine advertising, undated and 1904–1968; p. 4: *Munsingwear News,* August 1919, p. 9 [this issue is not part of the library's collection]; p. 11: Correspondence files, [ca. 188-]–1895; p. 29: Investigative Reports, Burns Detective Agency; p. 32, 52, 69, 70: Advertising and sales promotion, Photographs; p. 88: Vassarette materials; p. 95: Advertising and sales promotion, Printed materials, Hollywood Vassarette: Advertising and 1964–65.

Available online
p. 6–7: patents, Google.com/patents; p. 92: "Let's Get Down to Business," www.flicker.com

Photographs
p. 8 top: Edmund A. Bush; p. 15, Hibbard and Potter; p. 24 top, Charles P. Gibson; 37, 31, 44, 46–51, Charles J. Hibbard; 68, Norton & Peel. Photographers were not recorded for images on pages 8 bottom, 9 top, 12, 13, 21, 23, 24 bottom, and 26.

Reference Library
p. 34: *Munsingwear News,* January 1919, p. 9; p. 40: *Munsingwear News,* May 1921, p. 18–19; p. 42: *Munsingwear News,* September/October 1921, p. 29; p. 75: *The Curtain Rises on Munsingwear Modes* (Minneapolis: The Company, [1920]); p. 96, 97: Munsingwear, Inc., *Hollywood Vassarette Lingerie and Sleepwear* (Minneapolis: The Company, [1963]).

Munsingwear®